MW00888263

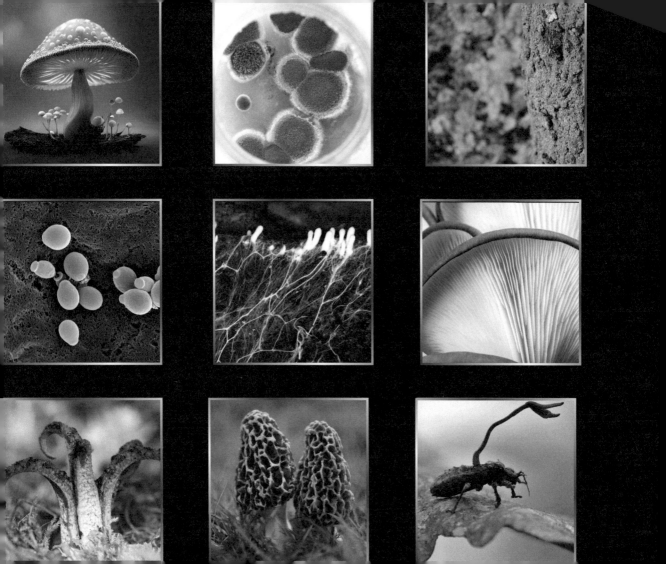

THE
ENCHANTED
FOREST

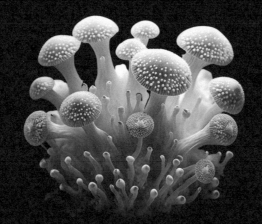

COPYRIGHT © ALL RIGHTS RESERVED.

BY HANS - JOACHIM KUHLMANN, BIOLOGIST, FOUNDER OF HK
& SONJA-MARIA MATTILA, BIOLOGIST

THE ENCHANTED FOREST

FOREST

MUSHROOM BIOLOGY FOR BEGINNERS & KIDS

HANS J. KUHLMANN

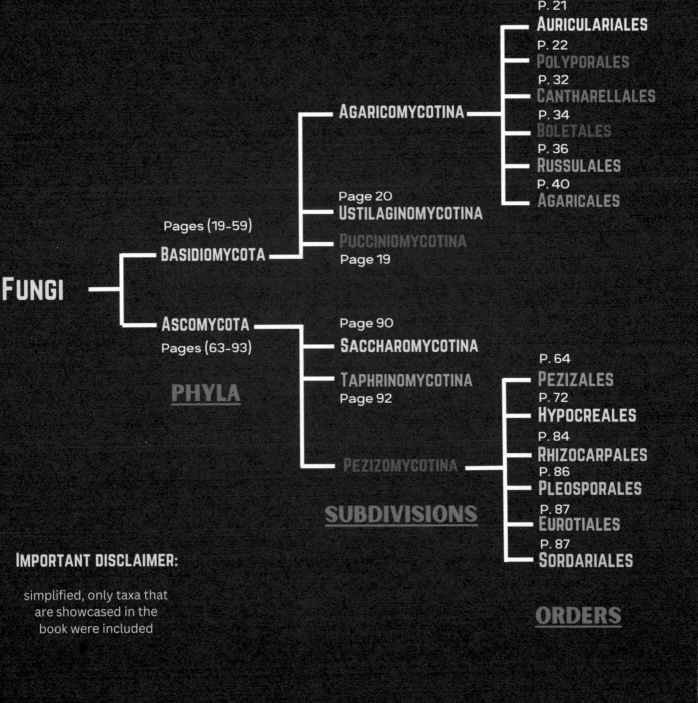

FUNGI

BASIDIOMYCOTA
Pages (19–59)

AGARICOMYCOTINA

Page 20
USTILAGINOMYCOTINA

PUCCINIOMYCOTINA
Page 19

ASCOMYCOTA
Pages (63–93)

Page 90
SACCHAROMYCOTINA

TAPHRINOMYCOTINA
Page 92

PEZIZOMYCOTINA

PHYLA

SUBDIVISIONS

ORDERS

IMPORTANT DISCLAIMER:

simplified, only taxa that
are showcased in the
book were included

SHORTCUTS

22

32

34

48

50

67

68

79

72

FOREWORD

We do not take any responsibility for harvesting decisions. This book is NOT a harvesting guide. Be always careful when approaching mushrooms, especially when uncertain what you're dealing with.

We felt that including references to studies, websites, and books we used for our research was inappropriate, for this book is meant for beginners and kids.

The family tree you will find in this book merely represents the families included in this book rather than a conclusive, final version of the entire fungal kingdom. The lines between each family do not represent monophyletic or paraphyletic relationships. They serve the purpose of visualization and categorization.

Controversial families, namely the psilocybes, have been covered in a non-biased manner to educate, not to enforce an agenda.

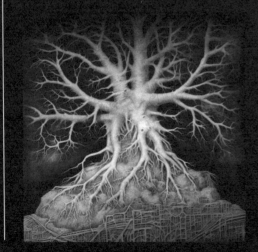

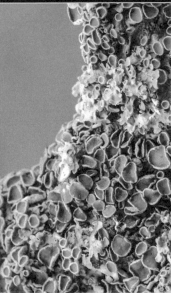

The Yellow Scale *(Xanthoria parietina)* occurs in forests all over the world. Mainly in hardwood forests in North America, Europe, Africa, Asia and Australia.

Fun Fact:

"What is this thing?" you're probably wondering. Some of you might even know "That's lichen!" But very few know that lichen is half fungus. Lichen is a symbiosis of Algae and Fungi.

A Symbiosis is a long-term interaction between two different organisms - However! it doesn't have to be a nice one, where both sides benefit or are unharmed.

Welcome to the first pages. This book is packed with beautiful illustrations collected from mushroom lovers worldwide. Attributions can be found at the back of the book.

We did our best to keep it as entertaining and straightforward as possible while providing a challenge and ensuring everyone has learned something new.

The following pages will take you on a ride through the entire fungal kingdom (or at least the juicy parts) while carefully introducing the difficult Latin and English names of the families and species in them.

The book doesn't have to be read in order. Feel free to use the content tree and jump straight to the stuff you're most curious about.

However, some biological terms and concepts are explained only once, so if you find yourself confused with a term, it was certainly explained earlier in the book.

We did our best to bring this usually misunderstood but wonderful and mysterious kingdom to life.

FUNGAL
PHYLOGENY

A fancy term for family history. When biologists talk about phylogeny, they mean the past of the 'group' they are talking about. The evolutionary history.

What groups and families do fungi occur in? What are their names? Find out on the next pages.

SO WHAT'S A MUSHROOM AND WHAT'S A FUNGUS?

You're probably wondering... *"What's a fungus and what's a mushroom?"*

Let me clear the air.

The mushroom is merely a reproductive organ also called a 'fruiting body.' Comparable to when a plant grows a flower. One of the differences is, that flowers are supposed to grab attention. Mushrooms aren't. That's primarily because flowers need pollinators to deliver their pollen to flowers of the opposite gender. Mushrooms have spores

The term fungi describes the whole fungal kingdom, including the fungi, which do not grow fruiting bodies during their reproductive stages.

Similarly, plants that grow flowers are categorized as flowering plants.

Now you're probably wondering "What would a fungus without a mushroom look like?" Probably something like a spider web (see pictures).

Hyphae are long, thin as a thread, and branched structures, which collectively form a mycelium. Hyphae can do a bunch of crazy things. Be firm enough to drill through rock... or move. "No way." Yep.

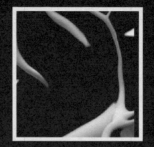
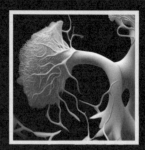
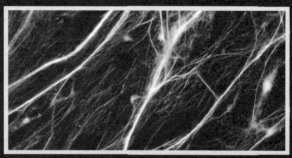

Featured: The main "body" of a fungus, called m*ycelium*. A very thin, intertwined web of root-like structures called *hyphae*".

They move by breaking down hyphae on one side of the mycelium, transporting the resources way back to the other side, and using them to grow new hyphae.

This process of nutrient redistribution is also called Translocation. Just a fancy word, you don't need to know this.

However, when it comes to speed, mycelium would make even a snail seem fast. Their speed reaches up to only a few millimeters a day!

Featured: A glowing mushroom (*Mycena chlorophos*), usually found in subtropical Asia (India, Japan, Taiwan...) and Brasil.

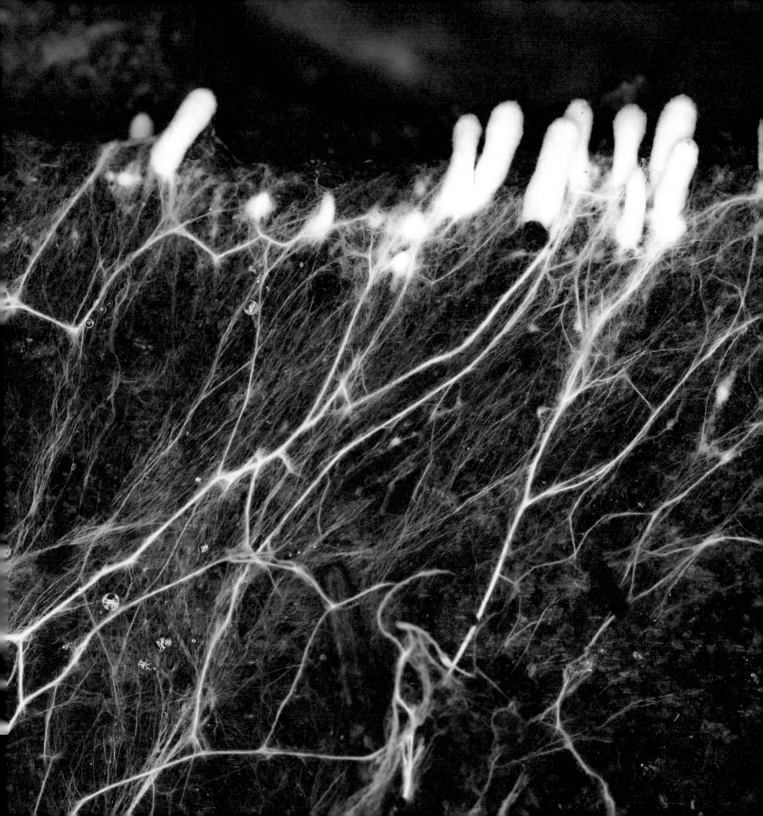

BASIDIOMYCOTA

Ah... Basidiomycota! The mushroom-bearing popular kid on the block. Most of the mushrooms you know and love will be in this taxon.

THE PHYLOGENETIC TREE

Fungi occur in 8 groups or the right term is 'Phyla' or "Taxa." Just like multiple chapters form a book, multiple Phyla form a kingdom. Five of them are considered 'major' phyla and were categorized based on their reproductive cycles or using advanced technology (molecular analysis - analysis of genes).

The most well-known phyla of the fungal kingdom are - Basidiomycetes & Ascomycetes, which form the subkingdom **Dikarya.**

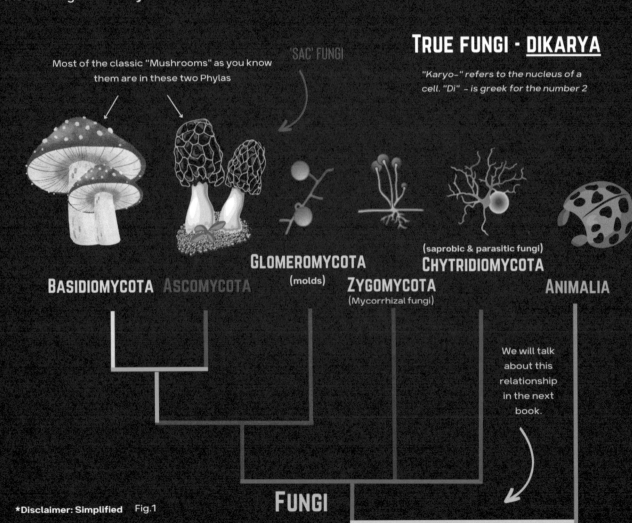

'SAC' FUNGI

Most of the classic "Mushrooms" as you know them are in these two Phylas

TRUE FUNGI - <u>DIKARYA</u>

"Karyo-" refers to the nucleus of a cell. "Di" - is greek for the number 2

GLOMEROMYCOTA
(molds)

(saprobic & parasitic fungi)
CHYTRIDIOMYCOTA

BASIDIOMYCOTA   **ASCOMYCOTA**

ZYGOMYCOTA
(Mycorrhizal fungi)

ANIMALIA

We will talk about this relationship in the next book.

FUNGI

COMMON ANCESTOR

*Disclaimer: Simplified   Fig.1

Featured: A mold fungus from the phylum *Zygomycota* and the order *Mucorales*, can be found on decomposing vegetables, leaves and wood.

Mushroom forming fungi.

BASIDIOMYCOTA

AGARICOMYCOTINA
jelly, coral, and shelf fungi
puffballs and stinkhorns.

PUCCINIOMYCOTINA
rusts

USTILAGINOMYCOTINA
smuts

BASIDIOMYCOTA ———————— **PUCCINIOMYCOTINA**
Phylum   Class

RUSTS - PUCCINIOMYCOTINA

Are plant pathogens (a microorganism, which causes disease) of the order *Pucciniales*.
They grow inside the cells of their hosts (intracellularly – inside the cells).

'Hosts' are the "victims" of parasites and pathogens (you are the host of a tick when you have one).

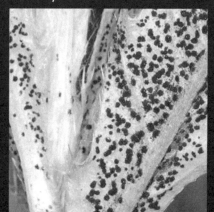

These 'groups' are also called taxons.

"Hey bro, what taxon is Basidiomycota?"

"A phylum, obviously."

KINGDOM
PHYLUM
CLASS
ORDER
FAMILY
GENUS
SPECIES

Just a little side-note, because I used order and class already twice.

When it comes to growing things and agriculture, rusts are a *huge* interference. So in example wheat stem rust, coffee bean rust, soybean rust and white pine blister rust are some of the infamous ones.

▲ Featured: A pear rust (*Gymnosporangium sabinae*), found on pear and juniper trees all over the world.

19

BASIDIOMYCOTA - SMUTS

BASIDIOMYCOTA ———— **USTILAGINOMYCOTINA**
Phylum   Class

SMUTS - (VARIOUS FAMILIES)

Smuts are a group of fungi that are harmful to plants (plant pathogens) and have a considerable impact on the economy. Similar to rusts they also infect essential crops like maize, barley, wheat, oats, and sugarcane.

These fungi produce **teliospores**, which are dark and sooty in appearance, and create powdery masses that resemble dirt or ash, hence the name "smuts."

Corn smut (*Ustilago maydis*) is

...in some countries considered a delicacy. So in example: Mexico.

it is called Huitlacoche and is a versatile ingredient that can be used in various dishes, such as soups, stews, steak sauces, and crepes.

"What are **spores?**" you're probably wondering.

Think of them as pollen in plants, or seeds in fruits (keyword: **reproduction**).

A spore drops on a suitable substrate, germinates, grows out hyphae, and eventually, it will mature into a mushroom.

Wild rice smut (*Ustilago esculenta*) grows on a variety of grasses (if you didn't know, rice is a grass too), hence on the picture a rice smut infection.

Rusts and Smuts are one of the reasons why we invented **fungicides**.
Considered a plague by many, except the Mexicans who found some good in the bad.

BASIDIOMYCOTA - JELLY FUNGI

BASIDIOMYCOTA
Phylum

AGARICOMYCOTINA
Class

AURICULARIALES
Order

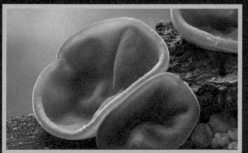

Auricula Auricula-Judae
Also known as the "Jelly Ear", "Juda's Ear" or "Jew's Ear," of which the latter was a mistranslation into the English language. There is a common belief that the fungus is linked to Judas Iscariot due to the notion that he hung himself on an elder tree following his betrayal of Jesus Christ.

AURICULARIES - JELLY FUNGI

A group of fungi that are characterized by their gelatinous texture. They can be found growing on logs, branches, and even on the ground.

They belong to the subphylum Agaromycotina in different classes: Dacrymycetales, **Auriculariales**, Sebacinales, and **Tremellales**.

Tremella fuciformis also known as the "Snow Fungus." Due to its snow-like appearance.

Has anti-inflammatory properties (cultivated and used in Chinese medicine). It reduces wrinkles and is a good source of vitamin D.

Ascocoryne sarcoides, or also "Purple Jellydisc." Grows on trees and protects the tree from infection by other rot fungi.

Contains **ascocorynin**, an antibioticum that inhibits the growth of some bacteria (more is not known).

Tremella mesenterica, or "witch's butter","yellow brain", "golden jelly fungus".

Can form symbiotic relationships with other fungi. For example with the notorious *Armillaria spp.* (the honey fungus).

Tremella absorbs the nutrients released during the decomposition of substrate (break down of organic matter) by the honey fungus.

This mushroom also is used in Chinese medicine. One could say they love jelly!

▲ Featured: The Golden Ear fungus (*Naematelia aurantia/Tremella aurantia*)

BASIDIOMYCOTA - POLYPORALES

BASIDIOMYCOTA
Phylum

AGARICOMYCOTINA
Class

*Disclaimer: Simplified

POLYPORALES

AURICULARIALES

POLYPORALES - POLYPORES, CORAL AND AGARIC FUNGI

Polyporales, also called shelf-fungi, is one of the largest orders in the basidiomycetes. It covers around 2000 species all over the world. Most are saprotrophic ("sapro" - Greek for "rotten," decomposers of dead organic material). Some are parasitic and will cause decay in live trees. Polypores are poroid fungi, meaning most have pores and tubes instead of gills on the underside of their caps

Their name stems from their shelf/bracket-like appearance, although some have a stem. You will often spot them growing out of trees or logs.

GANODERMATACEAE

POLYPORALES
Order

GANODERMATACEAE
Family

The Reishi Mushroom (the mushroom of immortality) has a long history in China as a spiritual mushroom.

Genus   Species
Ganoderma sichuanense is one of the most infamous mushrooms. With countless health benefits, also used in traditional Asian medicines, it is manufactured as a supplement all over the world.

1. Boosts immune system
2. Anti-cancer properties
3. Reduces fatigue
4. Helps with depression
5. Heart health
6. Diabetes Type 1 and 2
7. Improve sleep

Reishi is also used to build mushroom furniture, mycelium bricks and leather-like materials.

The Artist's Mushroom (*Ganoderma applanatum*)

Helps with:

1. Stomach pain and cramps
2. High blood pressure and cholesterol
3. Diabetes type I and II
4. Lung problems
5. Immune system problems
6. Cancer

Ganoderma applanatum, also called the artist's conk mushroom. It's unexpected feature lies in the fact it is used as an art medium. It's Japanese name is kofuki-saru-no-koshikake which means "powder-covered monkey's bench.

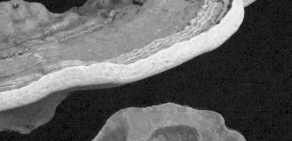

Fig. 2

Used to produce amadou.

Amadou is made from the inner layer of the mushroom. Its material is spongy in texture.

Amadou is used to start fires, make fabric for hats or to dry flies for fishing.

Fig. 3

Drawing on the underside of its cap.

Used in cooking because of its *umami* flavour.

Umami is one of the five tastes a human can taste : sweet, salty, sour, bitter, and umami (also called savory).

"Ötzi the Iceman" was a man who lived 5 000 years ago.

When Ötzi was found, frozen in ice, among other tools, he also carried a "hoof fungus" *Fomes fomentarius*, on his excursion through the Alps (mountainous area in Europe).

Similarly, *Fomes fomentarius* is also used to produce Amadou.

Hence it is suspected Ötzi carried the mushroom to start fires in the blistering cold.

BASIDIOMYCOTA - FOMITOPSIS

FOMITOPSIDACEAE

POLYPORALES	GANODERMATACEAE
	FOMITOPSIDACEAE

The genus 'Fomitopsis' consists of more than 40 species of bracket fungi. Of which most are brown-rot fungi, meaning, when they infect trees, their mycelium has a brown color.

FOMITOPSIS

The red-belted conk
(*Fomitopsis pinicola*)

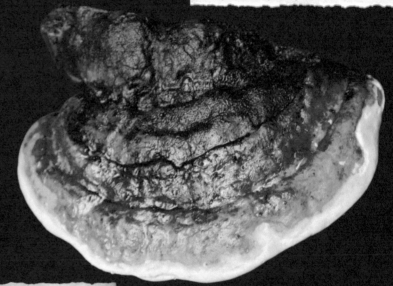

On the photo above can be seen the brown-rot inside the tree, caused by *Fomitopsis pinicola*.

Fungi vary in the color of their mycelium. Some black, some white, some brown, some yellow... yes, even pink.

Their color and other traits can be used for identification & categorization purposes.

1. Anti-inflammatory
2. Anti-bacterial
3. Anti-cancer
4. Anti-hemorrhoid
5. Anti-rheumatic

Traditionally, in folk medicine, sliced up into thin slices, Fomitopsis has been dunked into teas in North America, Europe and Russia for thousands of years, because of its antibacterial and nutritious value. Food wasn't so easy to come around back in the day.

24

▲ Featured: The Chaga mushroom "*Inonotus obliquus*," known for its white rot, despite its black charcoal-like appearance on the outside.

BASIDIOMYCOTA - FOMITOPSIS

Agarikon, also called Eburiko or Quinine conk
(Fomitopsis officinalis)

Fomitopsis officinalis,

an endangered species. Can be found only in old-growth forests (also called primary forests, forests with very little disturbance).

Unconventionally, this mushroom has been used by indigenous people to carve shamanistic masks and produce textiles.

Fig. 4

Has shown to help with:

1. Pox viruses
2. Herpes HSV-1 & HSV-2
3. Influenza A, Influenza B
4. Tuberculosis

It was also used in ancient Greece as medicine, to treat tuberculosis and natives for smallpox.

Hence the latin suffix "officinalis," which hints at the medicinal properties of the species.

Old-growth forests are basically biological libraries filled with important, ancient species.

Their protection is crucial in maintaining biodiversity and the development of new medicines in face of viruses and bacterial infections.

POLYPORACEAE

Are a family of poroid fungi. Some tough as bark, some tender as sponge. Most have white spores. The family consists of 78 diverse genera. Not much is known of this family, however, let yourself be treated with a variety of pictures.

POLYPORALES ———

- GANODERMATACEAE
- FOMITOPSIDACEAE
- LAETIPORACEAE
- **POLYPORACEAE**

| (no English name) *Lentinus berteroi* | (no English name) *Lentinus tigrinus* | Umbrella polypore *(Polyporus umbellatus)* |

Fig. 8

Fig. 9

| Sweet knot *(Globifomes graveolens)* | (no English name) *Microporus affinis* | Cinnabar polypore *(Pycnoporus cinnabarinus)* |

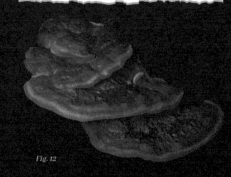

Fig. 10

Fig. 11

Fig. 12

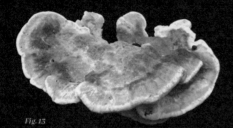

Fig. 13

(no English name)
Tryomyces galactinus

Fig. 14

Dryad's saddle
Cerioporus squamosus

Fig. 15

The Honeycomb mushroom
(*Favolus tenuiculus*)

This mushroom is the real deal. It packs a punch not only with its looks but also as a supplement.

Earning its name. Versicolor stands for "many colors," similar to those of a turkey. Hence, the English name, Turkey-tail Mushroom.

Microporus xanthopus

1. Boosts immunity
2. Improved cognitive function
3. Increased exercise performance
4. Improved gut health
5. Reduced inflammation
6. Lower blood sugar for type II diabetes

Used, clinically, in Japan to treat cancer. Paul Stamets, renowned mycologist, reported significant improvement in his mothers' stage 4 breast cancer, attributing her recovery to the supplementation with this mushroom.

Turkey-Tail Mushroom
(*Trametes versicolor*)

Birch polypore (*Fomitopsis betulina*)

Rosy conk (*Fomitopsis cajanderi*)

Fomitopsis spraguei
(has no English name)

BASIDIOMYCOTA - LAETIPORUS

Laetiporus

The genus 'Laetiporus' consists of mostly edible, bracket fungi. They are, for the most part, parasitic, meaning they exploit other organisms. In this case, trees, and similar to *Fomitopsis*, produce brown rot.

Polyporales
- Ganodermataceae
- Fomitopsidaceae
- Laetiporaceae

Chicken of the woods (*Laetiporus sulphureus*)

Another infamous mushroom.
The chicken-of-the-woods,
the crab-of-the-woods,
sulphur polypore, the list goes on.

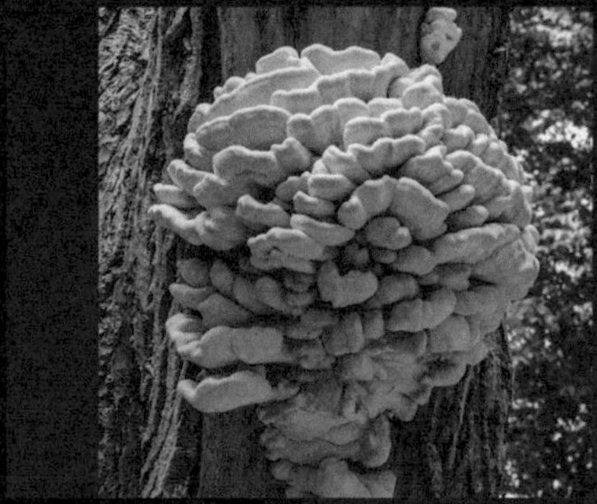

Fig.7

The Guinness world record holds an edible mushroom with the weight of 45 kg or 99 pounds.

Considered a delicacy, earning its name by the resemblance of taste to chicken when cooked.

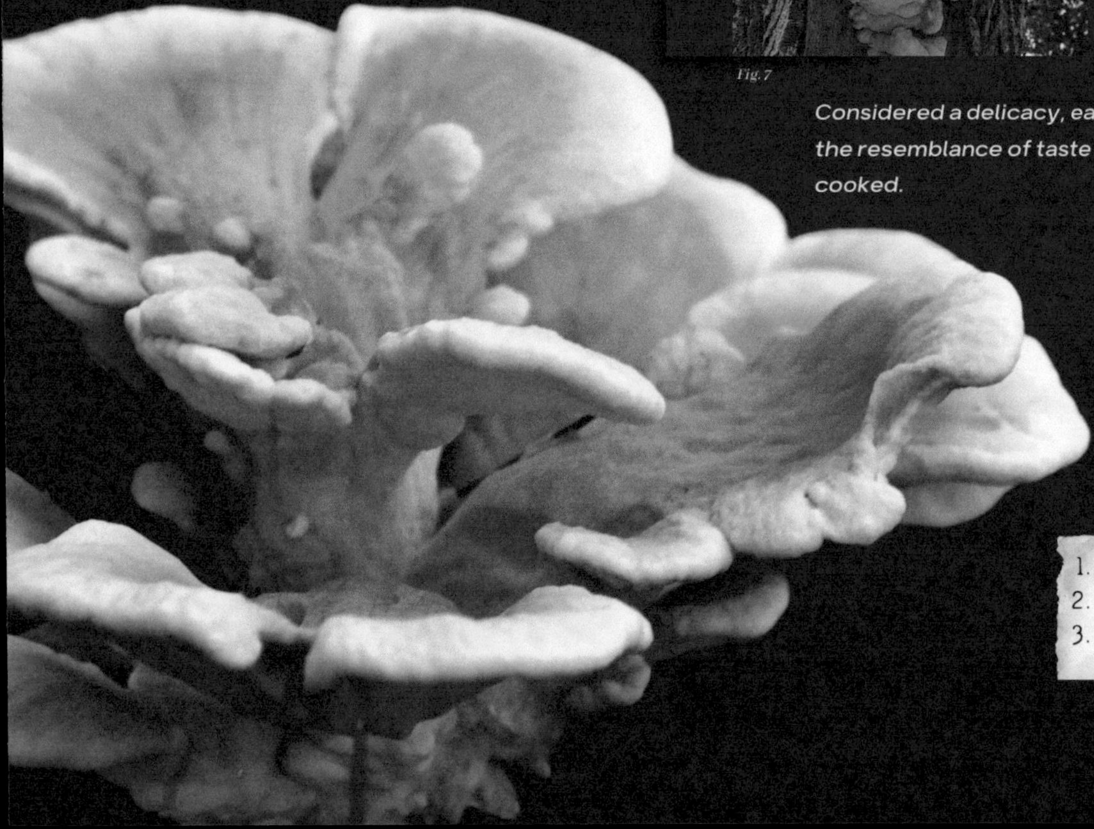

Widely distributed across Europe, North America (Rockies)

1. Anti-tumor
2. Anti-inflammatory
3. Rich in antioxidants

The mushroom above is known as yellowfoot or the winter mushroom (*Craterellus tubaeformis*). It is a mycorrhizal fungi. It grows in colder climates, mostly in northern Europe, North America, Russia and the Himalayas.

It is an excellent food mushroom and is used in soups and salads or fried.

BASIDIOMYCOTA — **AGARICOMYCOTINA**
Phylum   Class

Disclaimer: Simplified

- **AURICULARIALES**
- **POLYPORALES**
- **CANTHARELLALES**

CANTHARELLALES - CHANTERELLES

A pretty diverse order of fungi, not in terms of the number of species but in terms of appearances and lifestyles. Some are ectomycorrhizal, some are saprotrophic, and some are plant pathogens (I hope you can remember all of the terms, but I'd rather challenge you a bit than bore you). However, chantarelles are not known for their diversity, but rather for their culinary lucrativeness.

CANTHARELLALES ——— **CANTHARELLACEAE**

CANTHARELLACEAE

CANTHARELLACEAE ——— **CHANTARELLUS**

Grows only in Europe, from Scandinavia to the Mediterranean. However, other species from the same genus can be found worldwide. Mostly found in coniferous forests.

1. Anti-inflammatory
2. Bone health
3. Boost immunity

Golden chanterelle
(*Chantarellus cibarius*)

CRATERELLACEAE

CANTHARELLALES		CANTHARELLACEAE
		CRATERELLACEAE

Horn-of-plenty (*Craterellus cornucopioides*)

On the photo above can be seen the horn-of-plenty, black chanterelle, black trumpet or trumpet-of-the-dead (*Craterellus cornucopioides*).

Horn-of-plenty refers to the horn of 'Amalthea's' goat (a greek goddess), that filled itself with the drink or meat that was desired.

Grows in Europe, North America and East Asia.

The name 'black trumpet' may stem from the belief that dead people played the mushrooms from below the ground.

The white coral fungus or crested coral fungus (*Clavulina cristata*) is a species in the family of chantarellaceae, despite its drastically different fruiting body.

This shape of fruiting bodies is called 'clavarioid'.

Edible but not tasty.

Turkey-Tail Mushroom
(*Trametes versicolor*)

BASIDIOMYCOTA - BOLETALES

BOLETALES

Boletes are known for their sponge like surface under their cap. They appear in a variety of different colors and different types of fruiting bodies such as gilled mushrooms and puffballs. Boletales contain more than 1300 species, 17 families and 96 genera (the plural form of genus). Boletales are often ectomycorrhizal, however some species are parasitic or saprotrophic.

BASIDIOMYCOTA
Phylum

BOLETALES ———
Order

AGARICOMYCOTINA
Class

BOLETACEAE
Family

*Disclaimer: Simplified

- **AURICULARIALES**
- **POLYPORALES**
- **CANTHARELLALES**
- **BOLETALES**

BOLETACEAE

A family of mushroom-forming fungi, which are sought after worldwide. When someone thinks of mushrooms, mostly they think of the porcino, the king bolete. A mushroom from the genus Boletus. (Which mushroom do you think of?)

BOLETUS

There are many delicious edible mushrooms in the genus of Boletus.

The King Bolete/Porcino
(*Boletus edulis*)

BASIDIOMYCOTA - PAXILLACEAE

BOLETALES ⊏ BOLETACEAE
RUBROBOLETUS
PAXILLACEAE

RUBROBOLETUS

The Satan's bolete (*Rubroboletus satanas*) is classified as a poisonous mushroom. However, its distinctive appearance and pungent fishy smell serve as clear warning signs, making it difficult to confuse with edible boletes when fully mature.

The Satan's Bolete (*Rubroboletus satanas*)

PAXILLACEAE

The Paxillaceae family is part of the Boletales order and consists of 9 genera with 78 species.

Some of these mushrooms belong to the Paxillus type, distinguished by having gills, while others are classified as the Gyrodon type and have pores under their cap.

Fig. 16

Brown-roll rim (Paxillus involutus)

A commonly found gilled mushroom in this family is *Paxillus involutus*. It is more closely related to mushrooms with pores, such as boletes, rather than other gilled mushrooms.

This species is poisonous to humans and can cause severe autoimmune reactions.

35

BASIDIOMYCOTA - RUSSULALES

BASIDIOMYCOTA
Phylum

AGARICOMYCOTINA
Class

*Disclaimer: Simplified

AURICULARIALES
POLYPORALES
CANTHARELLALES
BOLETALES
RUSSULALES
Order

RUSSULALES ━━━━━━━━ **RUSSULACEAE**
Order   Family

RUSSULACEAE - BRITTLEGILLS

The brittlegills consist of about 1700 species, 117 genera, and 13 families.

The order Russulales includes many different fruiting body types. Some of these are polypores, tooth fungi, and club fungi. Identification of the species can be almost impossible in the field.

The Sickener (*Russula emetica*)

Its name hints at the tummy aches one gets after consumption raw. Associated with conifers and pine.

The spore dust colours range from white to creamy orange.

RUSSULALES - LACTARIACEAE

RUSSULALES —— RUSSULACEAE ⌐ RUSSULA
L LACTARIUS

Lactarius fungi get their name from their attribute to release milk-like "latex" when cut or damaged. The amount and color of the milk varies with species as well as the age of the mushroom.

Found in Europe, Siberia, New Zealand and Australia.

The color and sometimes smell of the milk when in contact with air can be useful in identifying the mushrooms.

Lactarius turpis is not edible and is sugested to be carcinogenic

The Ugly Milk-Cap (*Lactarius turpis*)

This milky substance is called "Latex" or "Milk" but it is not really any of those.

The Woolly Milkcap can be found in North Africa, northern Asia, Europe and North America.

Has a peppery flavor and is consumed in Finland and Russia. However, eating the mushroom raw will result in high irritation of the digestive system. With many mushrooms it matters a lot how you cook it so that it would be edible!

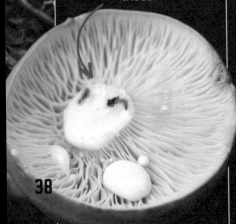

The Woolly Milkcap (*Lactarius torminosus*)

RUSSULALES - HERINACEAE

RUSSULALES —— RUSSULACEAE ⌐ RUSSULA
├ LACTARIUS
└ HERICIACEAE

HERICIACEAE

A family of species which are valued for their medicinal properties. They are saprobic and grow in northern temperate zones (below the polar but above the tropical zone).

Their distinctive feature is that they have spines or icicles hanging from their hymenium, such fruiting bodies are called hydnoid.

A hymenium is a layer of fungal tissue, usually under the cap, that holds spore producing cells (usually gilled or porous).

The Lion's Mane Mushroom (*Hericium erinaceus*)

Also called the bearded hedgehog or mountain-priest mushroom.

Not only medicinal, but also culinary.

On the picture above are neurons (brain-cells). Neurogenesis is a process during which new neural connections are formed and damaged connections repaired.

1. Anti-anxiety & depression
2. Protects the stomach
3. Reduces heart disease risks
4. Helps manage diabetes
5. Reduces inflammation
6. Boosts immune system
7. May help fight cancer
8. Induces neurogenesis

BASIDIOMYCOTA - AGARICALES

BASIDIOMYCOTA
Phylum

AGARICOMYCOTINA
Class

*Disclaimer: Simplified

- **AURICULARIALE**
- **POLYPORALES**
- **CANTHARELLALES**
- **BOLETALES**
- **RUSSULALES**
- **AGARICALES**
  Order

AGARICALES

Agaricales is recognized as one of the most diverse orders within the Basidiomycota phylum, encompassing a wide range of morphological variations across its 46 families, over 400 genera, and more than 25,000 identified species.

It is worth noting that Agaricales includes not only edible cultivated mushrooms but also some of the most toxic species in the entire fungal kingdom.

Recent advancements in DNA analysis have revolutionized our understanding of the phylogeny of Agaricales. These studies have revealed that not all gilled mushrooms are classified under Agaricales, whereas certain club, coral, and puffball fungi belong to this order.

AGARICALES —— AGARICACEAE

AGARICACEAE

Agaricaceae, a central family of *Agaricales*, has, similar to previous families, a number of species with varying fruiting body types.

Most *Agaricaceae* are saprotrophic, living in woodlands or grasslands.

As you have probably already noticed, many mushrooms have medicinal properties. The *Agaricaceae* family harbors numerous mushrooms with industrial, medicinal, or biotechnological importance. Further information about these mushrooms can be found on the next pages.

Oyster mushrooms are very important both in commercial and biotechnological fields.

Lycoperdaceae has been replaced to be a subgroup of Agaricaceae. Therefore in addition to the more common mushroom types the family of Agaricaceae includes also puffballs.

Spore prints **were used a lot in the studies of fungal diversity. Back in the day without molecular methods, that is.**
Placing a mushroom cap on black or white paper will reveal the color of its spores (white, creamy, yellow, green, purple. brown, rusty or black).

AGARICALES - PUFFBALLS

LYCOPERDON, CALVATIA · PUFFBALLS

Puffballs include multiple genera, such as Calvatia, Calbovista, and Lycoperdon. Their morphology is a unifying factor as they don't have a cap or outer spore-holding structures. Puffballs produce spores internally. The spores mature in the 'stomach of the puffball, and as the mushroom ages, it splits open from the top and releases the spores. Puffballs live in all kinds of woodlands living as saprophytes on dead organic matter

AGARICALES ——— AGARICACEAE ⊏ **AGARICUS**
LYCOPERDON
CALVATIA

Calvatia gigantea

Fig. 17

Puffballs come in different sizes and shapes. One of the largest ones is called Calvatia gigantea. It can grow to be as heavy as 44 pounds and have a diameter of 4,9 feet.

Lycoperdon curtisii

Also called wolf farts or devil's snuff box

Common puffball (*Lycoperdum perlatum*)

Puffballs were traditionally used in Tibet for ink making. They were burned and their ash was ground. To this ash, glue liquid and a decoction called "a nye shing ma" were added. The resulting solution was pressed for a long time until it formed a black, hard substance that was used as ink.

Since the discovery of the medicinal benefits of puffballs by Native Americans, extensive scientific research has confirmed the antibacterial, antifungal, and antimicrobial properties of their spores. These spores show promising potential in combatting differetn diseases such as staph infections, salmonella, and E.coli.

Native American tribes have long relied on puffballs for various purposes. They found them helpful for treating wounds by combining the spores with spiderwebs and bark, and applying this mixture to stop bleeding. Puffballs were also used to alleviate sores and burns.

Different tribes had different uses for puffballs. Some gathered them as a source of food, while others wore them around their necks to ward off evil spirits. Occasionally, puffballs would grow in circular formations, now known as fairy circles. These circles were believed to be formed by fallen stars during supernatural events. Dried puffballs were also useful for starting fires, and they were seen as a special gift from nature. As a result, they were often depicted on tipi canvases to symbolize the strength of a warm and comforting fire.

The Portobello (*Agaricus bisporus*)

AGARICALES - AGARICUS

AGARICALES ——— AGARICACEAE

AGARICACEAE ——— AGARICUS

AGARICUS

The Agaricus genus consists of both edible and poisonous species. Among the most commonly consumed edible mushrooms are those belonging to the Agaricus genus, including Portobello, the horse mushroom, the field mushroom, and the almond mushroom. Some of these mushrooms have also been suggested to possess medicinal benefits.

However, there have been concerns regarding their potential adverse effects on the liver. Therefore, it is crucial to conduct thorough research and studies to better understand the potential risks and benefits.

The portobello, *Agaricus bisporus*, is a worldwide cultivated mushroom .

The yellow-stainer
(*Agaricus xanthodermus*)

Be cautious to not mistake edible Agaricus mushrooms for some poisonous agaricus mushrooms or amanita mushrooms such as one of the deadliest mushrooms *Amanita phalloides*.

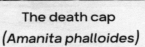

The death cap
(*Amanita phalloides*)

AGARICALES- PLEUROTACEAE

Pink Oyster Mushroom
(*Pleurotus djamor*)

AGARICALES —— AGARICACEAE
└── PLEUROTACEAE

PLEUROTACEAE —— PLEUROTUS

PLEUROTACEAE

The Pleurotaceae family, also known as the tree mushroom family, lives on dead wood. They are saprotrophic, but also nematophagous.
(Got an idea what that means?)

It means that they consume nematodes and obtain nutrition and nitrogen from them (carnivores, yes).

Tastes like bacon or ham.

PLEUROTUS

A genus of globally cultivated & consumed mushrooms. Considered to be of high gastronomic and biotechnological value. Oyster mushrooms grow on a wide variety of substrates, and have shown impressive heavy metal and oil absorption properties.

Use of mushrooms in an attempt to regenerate an ecosystem is termed as mycoremediation.

They grow in a wide variety of climates, from tropical to temperate forests around the globe.

These carnivores have different strategies to catch their prey. The Pleurotus mushrooms use nematotoxic poison to stun the roundworms. After this, they wrap their hyphae around the worm to degrade it with enzymes. Some mushrooms have sticky knobs in their hyphae which trap the by-passing worms. Some mushrooms in the Pleurotaceae family are parasites. They attach their sticky spores to the worm, and as the spores germinate, they pierce through the worm and start growing on it.

Golden Oyster Mushroom
(*Pleurotus citrinopileatus*)

Can be grown at home.

The king oyster is a mushroom that grows in the Mediterranean and Asia.

It is critically endangered and currently there are no rules prohibiting the harvesting of immature individuals.

King Oyster
(*Pleurotus eryngii*)

HEALTH BENEFITS

1. Anti-tumor
2. Anti-oxidant benefits
3. Heart health
4. Lowers cholesterol
5. Blood sugar regulation
6. Immune system support
7. Gut health

Phoenix Mushroom
(*Pleurotus pulmonarius*)

Can be found in the eastern US and in most tropical and temperate forests.

Tastes like bitter almonds.

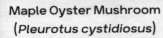

Fig. 21

Maple Oyster Mushroom
(*Pleurotus cystidiosus*)

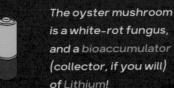

The oyster mushroom is a white-rot fungus, and a bioaccumulator (collector, if you will) of Lithium!

The maple oyster mushroom is edible at choice and is cultivatable, very little is known about this mushroom.

It is a global delicacy, found in many different dishes in Japan, Slovakia, Germany...

Oyster mushrooms are used for the production of mycelial bricks and mycelial furniture.

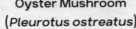

Oyster Mushroom
(*Pleurotus ostreatus*)

A few genera from the Agaricaceae family, namely Leucoagaricus and Leucocoprinus, are cultivated by fungus-growing ants. These ants have a mutualistic relationship with the fungi, as they help them to spread their spores and, in turn, receive food.

It is hypothesised that the ants are protected from bacteria by the fungal antibacterial properties.

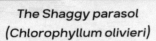

The Shaggy parasol
(Chlorophyllum olivieri)

MACROLEPIOTA

The *Macrolepiota* genus consists of common white-spored mushroom species in the Agaricaceae family.

The most known and utilized one from the genus is the Parasol mushroom, Macrolepiota procera. They are saprobic, which means they grow on organic matter, usually in environments lacking oxygen.

The parasol mushroom is not only a delicious and nutritious alternative for meat, but its medicinal properties have been made use of in treatments for diabetes, high blood pressure and inflammations.

When distinguishing gilled and scale-capped Macrolepiota mushrooms, it is important to be cautious and avoid confusing them with potentially deadly Chlorophyllum mushrooms.

The most eaten poisonous mushroom is the Chlorophyllum olivieri.

AGARICACEAE	AGARICUS
	LYCOPERDON
	CALVATIA
	MACROLEPIOTA

The Parasol mushroom
(*Macrolepiota procera*)

1. Anti-inflammatory
2. Bone health (vitamin D)
3. Boost immunity
4. Diabetes

CLAVARIACEAE

AGARICALES
- **AGARICACEAE**
- **PLEUROTACEAE**
- **CLAVARIACEAE**

The *Clavariaceae* family includes a huge variety of different interesting fruiting bodies including branched coral-like structures and jelly-like forms.

Camarophyllopsis sp.

Fig. 19

Mucronella pendula is one of the less common hydnoid fungi in Clavariacee. It has a pendant/spine type fruiting body.

Mucronella pendula

Fig. 18

Most clavariaceae species are biotrophs (they grow on living plant matter). However Hirticlavula elegans is a saprotroph and lives on dead organic matter. Its fruiting bodies grow only as big as 1.1 mm (0.04 inches).

Hirticlavula elegans

Fig. 20

Clavariaceae includes a lot of coral fungi that have a branched, antler-like shape and a rubbery texture.

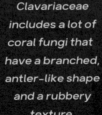

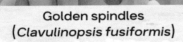

Golden spindles
(*Clavulinopsis fusiformis*)

The Violet coral
(*Clavaria zollingeri*)

49

AGARICALES - AMANITACEAE

The *Amanita* genus includes some of the most *deadly mushrooms* in the fungal kingdom. *Amanita virosa* is a prime example of these toxic mushrooms. It is one of the white Amanita mushrooms also called "*destroying angels*".

The Violet coral (Amanita virosa)

AGARICALES ⟶ AGARICACEAE
PLEUROTACEAE
CLAVARIACEAE
AMANITACEAE

AMANITACEAE

Amanitaceae is a mushroom-forming family, of which most are ectomycorrhizal (you know what that means by now, wink), forming mutual relationships, usually with oaks and conifers.

There are a few edible and tasty mushrooms, but also deadly poisonous ones. Species of this family are the reason for more than half of the mushroom poisonings.

The Toadstool, Fly Agaric (Amanita muscaria)

AMANITA

Amanita is one of the most well-known genera of mushrooms. I am pretty sure you know the name of this flamboyant species.

Despite its tasty look, Fly agaric is poisonous. However, rarely people die as a consequence of its consumption.

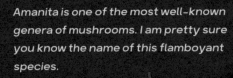

BASIDIOMYCOTA - AMANITA'S MYTHS

The Kamchadales and Koryaks of Siberia are indigenous tribes around the Arctic Circle, known for herding reindeer.

The story tells that on the night of the winter solstice, the Koryak shamans would collect Fly Agaric (which grows almost exclusively under pine trees), hang it from branches (or in a sock), and dry it over a fire (Does that sound familiar?)

Why? Because dried or cooked Fly Agaric is psychoactive and can evoke religious and spiritual experiences.

Furthermore, they would wear red outfits with white dots in honor of the mushroom's colors, and because of the deep snow, they'd wear tall boots of reindeer skin, which were blackened by exposure over time.

The shamans would return from their gathering trips back to the village with a sack filled with mushrooms. The villages were built with 'yurts', houses with wide holes in the middle of their roof.

This is where other high-ranking tribe members were waiting for the shamans to return with the sack of mushrooms.

However, with a lot of snow around the cottage, they were forced to climb up the yurt and jump down from above the fireplace. Some say that a pole was raised so that the shaman could slide down.

This is how some people believe Christmas has come to be.

As with all myths, their source is difficult to find and prove its validity, thus, this story remains just an interesting myth. However, who knows, maybe there is some truth to it!

However, beyond the hallucinations, the mushrooms stimulate the muscular system as well, and to such extent, that reindeer (Rangifer tarandus) which consumed them, would be affected by a surge of energy that would make them all high and mighty. Often jumping so high, that it might appear they were flying. Not to mention, that the humans who observed them were also high, obscuring their judgment.

AGARICALES - COPRINUS

Coprinus

Coprinus species are more commonly known as 'Ink Caps'. The name refers to the black, inky fluid that drips out of the aged fruiting bodies. The liquid contains the spores of the mushroom.

The Ink Caps are relatively short-lived mushrooms. They will emerge from the ground in one night and decompose again in the next two days. Another notable feature is the elongation of the mushroom's stem as it ages. It can grow 5 to 6 times the original height within a few hours.

The Shaggy Ink Cap
(*Coprinus comatus*)

A young Shaggy ink cap is an appreciated delicacy in cooking. In addition to its great content of important minerals and proteins, it also has medicinal components. It has been shown to help deal with obesity, bowel functions, and blood circulation. It has also shown potential in treating type I and II diabetes.

CORTINARIACEAE

At least 34 species in the *Cortinariacea* family contain one and the same toxin: Orellanine. The toxin seems to have different kinds of effects not only on animals but also on plants and microorganisms.

AGARICALES ——— CORTINARIACEAE
CORTINARIACEAE ——— CORTINARIUS

CORTINARIUS

Cortinarius is the biggest genus in the *Cortinariaceae* family. There is not many edible cortinarius species. However, some have been used as natural dyes to color wool yarn and fabrics as their fruiting bodies contain a lot of pigments (in water insoluble colors).

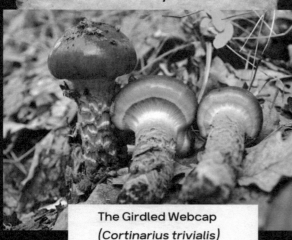

The Girdled Webcap
(*Cortinarius trivialis*)

The Violet Webcap
(*Cortinarius violaceaus*)

1:1 portion of mushrooms and fiber can be gently boiled in water for 1/2 - 1 h. The dyeing properties of mushrooms vary and therefore the results can also be very different.

Handling poisonous mushrooms can cause irritation or other toxin reactions also through skin, eyes and respiratory system.

The mushroom above is known as Verdigris agaris (Stropharia aeruginosa). It is a slimy woodland mushroom. Its edibility is in dispute. Some claim it is edible, and some say it is poisonous. However, its effects are little known, and its toxins have not been researched well enough yet.

STROPHARIACEAE

Strophariaceae is another family under the order of Agaricales. It includes about 18 genera and 1316 species of which all are saprotrophs.

They have red-brown to dark-brown spores which turn the older mushrooms' cap dark underneath.

STROPHARIA

The genus Stropharia is the biggest subgroup of Strophariaceae. You might know it by the name 'roundheads'. They all have a ring on the stem.

The Wine cap stropharia or the Garden giant or King's stropharia (Stropharia rugosoannulata) is native to Europe and North America. It can grow up to 8 inches tall, with a cap up to 12 inches wide, hence, the name "Garden Giant".

It is an edible mushroom, considered a delicacy in some countries. The Garden giant is also perfect to grow in combination with corn.

It produces spiny cells called acanthocytes, which are able to immobilise and digest nematodes.

AGARICALES
- AGARICACEAE
- PLEUROTACEAE
- CLAVARIACEAE
- AMANITACEAE
- CORTINARIACEAE
- STROPHARIACEAE

Fig. 22

The Questionable Stropharia
(Stropharia ambigua)

STROPHARIACEAE ———— STROPHARIA

The Garden Giant
(Stropharia rugosannulata)

PHOLIOTA

Pholiota is another genus under the Strophariaceae family. Pholiota consists of around 150 species. Like other Strophariaceae species, they are also saprotrophs.

STROPHARIACEAE — STROPHARIA
                   PHOLIOTA

Flaming scalycap (Pholiota flammans)

The genus Pholiota consists of small to medium sized mushrooms that often have a scaly cap surface. The name pholiota refers to the Greek word 'pholis' "scale".

Pholiota adiposa is one of the edible pholiota mushrooms growing on trees as parasites or saprotrophs. The mushroom produces certain chemicals that have antitumor and antioxidant properties.

Fig. 23

Pholiota squarrosa has a parasitic nature, invading the tissue of living plants and trees. It has specific chemicals that it uses to neutralize the plants' defense mechanisms, such as the release of chemicals that are irritating to fungi.

The Pholiota nameko or just nameko (Pholiota microspora) is a species in the genus of Pholiota, standing out with its smooth and gelatinous appearance. It is Japan's most popular mushroom for cultivation and is used in miso soups and nabemono (pot dishes). It usually fruits in fall when temperatures drop below 50 degrees Fahrenheit (10 degrees Celsius). However, it is also sold in kit form for people to grow at home.

Chestnut Mushroom (Pholiota adiposa)

Pholiota squarrosa (Shaggy scalycap)

Magic mushrooms can be ingested dried, fresh and as a tea.

Magic mushrooms gave rise to psychedelic art, usually very colourful and alien-like, which is supposed to imitate the hallucinations one sees when under the influence of magic mushrooms.

HYMENOGASTRACEAE

A family of 17 genera and about 1300 species, some of which are false-truffle shaped and some agaric (caps with gills). The most infamous genus of all, probably, would be the *Psilocybes*.

AGARICALES	
	AGARICACEAE
	PLEUROTACEAE
	CLAVARIACEAE
	AMANITACEAE
	CORTINARIACEAE
	STROPHARIACEAE
	HYMENOGASTRACEAE

PSILOCYBE

Growing worldwide in most biomes, psilocybes can be found growing from under a cow patty or on wood chip mulch around urban areas.

Psilocybes are renowned for their blue discoloration when their tissue is damaged, due to the oxidation (A reaction of a compound with oxygen found in the surrounding air) of Psilocybin which it contains in its cells. (Although some don't blue!)

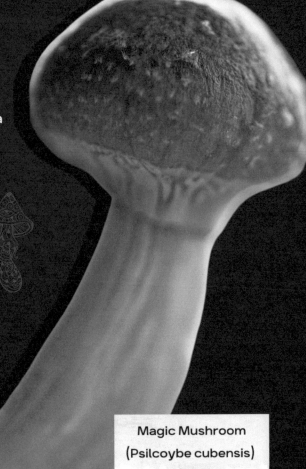

Magic Mushroom
(Psilcoybe cubensis)

MAGIC MUSHROOMS

Psilocybin is a psychedelicum which induces hallucinations, varying in degree determined by the dosage.

Microdosing is the application of magic mushrooms on a day-to-day basis, ingesting 1/10 of a small dose. (0,1g -> 1g) - which is reported to bring about increase in creativity and overall well-being.

Magic mushrooms are a risky business, in many countries over the world they are illegal.

Magic mushrooms are considered to be powerful tools, whose use has been dated back to ancient civilizations.

Dosages range from micro to macro, of which both have been tested in clinical trials and brought about interesting results.

Magic mushroom use is associated with ease in anxiety, mortal anxiety, depression and addiction.

Psychedelica such as mushrooms and LSD (derived from psilocybin) are non-addictive,

People prone to Schizophrenia and Neurosis should stay away from magic mushrooms, for they can trigger the onset of the mentioned diseases earlier.

Magic mushrooms were used in many cultures by shamans to induce spiritual and religious experiences, which start after ingestion of about 1 gram of dried psilocybe mushrooms. The higher the dose the more uncontrollable and potentially, scarier, the experience.

With high doses from 3-5g and above one can experience an ego death (the dissolution of ego) which feels pretty much like dieing.

Magic mushrooms are not to be considered as a fun thing to do, but as powerful healing tools which demand respect and awareness.

Many people report horrible experiences while under the influence of magic mushrooms.

AGARICALES - PHYSALACRIACEAE

AGARICALES ─────┐

- AGARICACEAE
- PLEUROTACEAE
- CLAVARIACEAE
- AMANITACEAE
- CORTINARIACEAE
- STROPHARIACEAE
- HYMENOGASTRACEAE
- **PHYSALACRIACEAE**

PHYSALACRIACEAE

Physalacriaceae is a very diverse mushroom family that can be found growing from the Arctic to the tropics. Most species in this family form fruiting bodies with a cap and a stem. However, also corticoid (patch-like) and secotioid (bag-shaped) species are included in this group.

The mushroom above is known as the Porcelain mushroom (Oudemansiella mucida).
It is a saprotrophic fungus growing mostly on rotting beech. The Porcelain fungus contains strong anti-fungal chemicals (fungicides), such as strobilurin that it uses to outcompete almost all other fungi from the area. This natural fungicide has been utilized in agriculture to protect crops from disruptive fungi.

Honey fungi (*Armillaria mellea*)

Armillaria (a genus in the Physalacriaceae family) are very long-lived fungi. The largest living fungi colony in the world is Armillaria ostoyae. Even though the fruiting bodies are rather tiny, a fungal colony of A. ostoyae found in the Blue Mountains of eastern Oregon is estimated to be 2400 years old and cover 2200 acres (8.9km^2) of area. There are also rough estimations of the weight of the fungal mass in that colony: 605 tons.

Wild "Enoki"
(*Flammulina velutipes*)

The enoki mushroom (Flammulina filiformis) is a well-known and important, widely cultivated edible mushroom in Japan. Its wild form looks much different from the cultivated one. During cultivation, the mushrooms are not exposed to light, which causes them to stay really white in comparison to the wild form.
Enoki is a great source of many B vitamins and phosphorus.

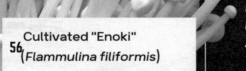

Cultivated "Enoki"
(*Flammulina filiformis*)

HYMENOCHETALES

Hymenochaetales are an order of fungi that contain around 600 species. The morphological features vary, comprised by fungi with mostly corticoid and poroid but also clavarioid and agaric fruiting bodies. The group inholds fungi of economic and therapeutic importance.

Most species in the order are saprotrophs of dead organic matter. However some cause rots of living trees causing forestry damage. Some are ectomycorrhizal and some are parasitic, living on mosses and liverworts.

The willow bracket
(Phellinus igniarius)

INONOTUS OBLIQUUS, 'CHAGA'

Inonotus obliquus belongs to the Hymenochaetaceae family, like the Phellinus iginarius. Inonotus obliquus is a parasitic fungus growing mostly on birch trees. Even though the burnt-looking conk is the most visible feature of the fungus, it is only a mineralized mass formed by the mycelium. It is not the fruiting body. The fungus might keep decaying the host tree for

10-80 years before it forms the actual fruiting body as the tree dies. Chaga has medicinal properties of lowering cholesterol, preventing and slowing cancer and supporting the immune system.

HEALTH BENEFITS

1. Anti cancer
2. Anti inflammatory
3. Lowers blood sugar
4. Anti diabetes
5. Lowers cholesterol

Phellinus fungi belong also into the Hymenochaetales order and hymenochaetaceae family. Phellinus is a genus of fungi which are mostly wood decaying species causing also damage to forests.

Phellinus species have been noticed to produce multiple natural chemicals that have different kinds of bio-active properties.

The Australian Aborigines have been using Phellinus mushrooms to treat cold symptoms such as sore throat and fever by either smoking or preparing it as a tea.

ASCOMYCOTA

If Basidiomycota are the popular, small brother...

Ascomycota are the weird, introverted, misunderstood big brother that no one talks about.

Instead of a cap with gills or pores, they develop 'sacs' filled with spores. Their reproductive cycles are... complex. They range from lichens to truffles.

ASCOMYCOTA

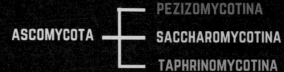

ASCOMYCOTA —[PEZIZOMYCOTINA
SACCHAROMYCOTINA
TAPHRINOMYCOTINA

Ladies and gents, Ascomycota or sac fungi, are by far the largest taxonomic group in the fungal kingdom, reaching up to 110 thousand species, the number increasing by the second. So in example, the current data on Wikipedia states that Ascomycota are comprised of 64 thousand species, however, in scientific journals one bumps into a number almost twice as big.

In comparison, 330 thousand species of plants are known to science, likewise 6 thousand species of mammals.

So what's so special about these little creatures? Besides their numbers.
Ascomycota differ from other fungi thanks to their development of an Ascus. An ascus is a cell (the smallest, functional unit of living organisms) that holds spores in it – mostly eight of them.

However, some sac fungi are asexual – which means – they produce clones.

A more extensive range of Ascomycota diversity would include – lichen, morels, truffles, yeasts (the stuff used, among other things, for beer brewing), cup fungi, and among molds – plant pathogens, insect pathogens, and human pathogens.

Spore bearing cell – Ascus

Sack

Spore

They release their spores by bursting their tip, or by slowly digesting themselves.

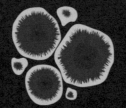

Ascomycota are split into three classes:
1. Pezizomycotina – by far the largest, most interesting class in the Ascomycota
2. Saccharomycotina – many of the yeasts are in this class
3. Taphrinomycotina – includes some plant pathogens and one order which produces fruiting bodies

The earliest fossil members of Pezizomycotina, the Paleopyrenomycites, have been dated to the Early Devonian Rhynie chert (fossils inholding sediment layer).

The Rhynie chert has been formed in the early stages of life moving from oceans to land. Some of the fossils have stayed in a remarkable condition, so much so that it is possible with a microscope to see how the fungal hyphae is growing into the plant tissue, working as a decomposer or a mycorrhizal symbiont.

PEZIZOMYCOTINA

Pezizomycotina is the biggest subdivision of *Ascomycota*. *Pezizomycotina* include most filamentous fungi that form a fruiting body.

ASCOMYCOTA
- PEZIZOMYCOTINA
- SACCHAROMYCOTINA
- TAPHRINOMYCOTINA

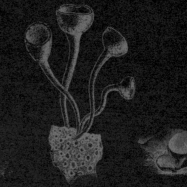

PEZIZOMYCOTINA ——— PEZIZOMYCETES ——— PEZIZALES

PEZIZALES

Pezizales are an order within Pezizomycotina that contains 16 families and 1683 species. Some of them are more familiar to us such as morels and truffles, some again more hidden and mysterious.

Pezizales species vary from saprobic to mycorrhizal and parasitic species. Pezizales morphology varies a lot between families.

The Orange peel fungus
(*Aleiuria aurantia*)

Most Pezizales fungi appear in temperate regions or at higher elevations, growing in acidic soil with little organic matter. A few species are tropical.

PEZIZACEAE

The *Pezizaceae* family is commonly referred to as "cup fungi" even though it is not the only cup-shaped family in the *pezizomycotina*.

The cup shape serves a purpose in spore dispersal. The curvature allows the wind to blow out the spores better. Also, raindrops splash the spores from the surface of the cup.

PEZIZALES ⎡ PEZIZACEAE
⎢ PYRONEMATACEAE
⎣ SACROSCYPHACEAE

The Bay Cup fungus
(*Peziza badia*)

The Eyelash cup
(*Scutellinia scutellata*)

PYRONEMATACEAE

Pyronemataceae is the largest family in the *Pezizales* order. Species in this family vary a lot in size and shape. They are brightly colored (as you saw with *Aleuria aurantia*) because they contain carotenoid pigments, the same as fruits and veggies have. (The name carotenoid stems from the fact carotenoids are found in carrots.)

SACROSCYPHACEAE

Sacroscyphaceae, the Elf Cups, and allies are found worldwide. They are saprotrophic, mainly growing on decaying wood.

All species of the *Sacroscypha* genus are on the red list of threatened species in Europe (a list made by the International Union for conservation of Nature). Cup fungi prefer to fruit during colder months, presenting a welcome food source for rodents and slugs.

The scarlet elf cup or the scarlet cup (Sacroscypha coccinea) has been used medicinally by the Oneuda people and possbly other tribes as well. The dried and pulverized scarlet cup was applied to bleeding wounds and under bandages as a styptic. Styptic agents contract the injured tissue and seal the blood vessels.

According to European folklore, the wood elves drink morning dew from the cups.

ASCOMYCOTA - DISCINACEAE

Discinaceae can be both epigeous and hypogeous (above - epi, and below -hypo, soil, basically)

Above ground, they produce saddle or bowl shaped fruiting bodies - apothecia.

Below ground they produce truffles.

DISCINACEAE

Discinaceae, is known to consist of six genera. A family most renowned for the false morels, the genus *Gyromitra*.

DISCINACEAE ——
- **DISCINA**
- **GYROMITRA**

DISCINA

Discina perlata or also known as pig's ears, can be found on decomposed organic material, or rotten wood in coniferous forests of North America.

PEZIZALES ——
- PEZIZACEAE
- PYRONEMATACEAE
- SACROSCYPHACEAE
- **DISCINACEAE**

GYROMITRA

Very common in Europe and North America, fruiting in coniferous forests under trees in spring. It has a brain-shaped cap, thanks to which it earned its name, the Brain Mushroom. Despite its toxicity, it is considered a delicacy in Finland. It is ingested after parboiling. It contains monomethylhydrazine (MMH, rocket fuel), which affects the CNS (central nervous system) and the liver.

developing meiotic asci

sterile hyphae

mature asci

Fig.24

Pig's Ears (*Discina perlata*)

For sale in Helsinki, with a don't touch sign.

Tarjous Korvasieni 10 €/kg

DON'T TOUCH!

Fig. 25

Brain Mushroom
(*Gyromitra esculenta*)

MORCHELLACEAE

The family of morels, Morchellaceae, contains 49 species in 4 genera. The family is mycorrhizal.

We still remember that genera, is the plural form of genus, right?)

The family is known for the true morels (*Morchella*), the thimble morels (*Verpa*) and cup-shaped fungi (*Disciotis*).

PEZIZALES
- PEZIZACEAE
- PYRONEMATACEAE
- SACROSCYPHACEAE
- DISCINACEAE
- MORCHELLACEAE

MORCHELLACEAE
- MORCHELLA
- VERPA
- DISCIOTIS

Early Morel (*Verpa conica*)

MORCHELLA

With a bunch of names, the morel (*Morchella esculenta*) is quite infamous and sought after by many bloated culinary sensualists. It grows under hardwood and conifers, but can also be found on land under fruit and nut trees.

(*Disciotis venosa*)

HEALTH BENEFITS

1. Anti-Tumor
2. Boost immunity
3. High in antioxidants
4. High in minerals
5. Strong teeth and bones
6. Protect liver

Their spores are not released spontaneously. Fungi with this type of cap had to develop new strategies of dispersal.

Cleistothecia, on the other hand, are fully closed which means,

They attract animals to consume their flesh and release their spores.

True Morel (*Morchella esculenta*)

ASCOMYCOTA- TUBERACEAE

Truffles are hard to find since they're underground. Pigs as well as dogs can be trained to be "trufflers." Pigs can find them innately, that's why they have to be trained, to not eat them when they do.

Dogs on the other hand, have to be trained to find them in the first place.

Fig. 26

TUBERACEAE

Truffles are, similarly to morels, mycorrhizal (ectomycorrhizal), which makes both families very difficult to cultivate, and hence very expensive on the market. Truffles are also called, "the diamond of the kitchen."

The truffle is a fruiting body, that grows -- underground, hypogeous, remember?

Despite Tuber being the genus that is considered the "true" truffle, there are over 100 other genera that produce hypogeous truffles (truffle-shaped fruiting bodies).

TUBER

This genus goes back to the Jurassic period. Sporting multiple species of truffles - white, black, burgundy...

PEZIZALES	PEZIZACEAE
	PYRONEMATACEAE
	SACROSCYPHACEAE
	DISCINACEAE
	MORCHELLACEAE
	TUBERACEAE

So what does the fact that a truffle is a fruiting body tell us about it?

1. Should have spores
2. Should be nutritious

Both are correct.

HEALTH BENEFITS

1. Anti-cancer
2. Antibacterial
3. Rich in antioxidants
4. Anti-inflammatory

Black truffle
(*Tuber melanosporum*)

ASCOMYCOTA- TUBERACEAE

Truffles can be cultivated, however, the effort which goes into doing so exceeds the expectations of initial enthusiasts.

Since they are mycorrhizal, trees, that are known to bear truffles under them are targeted, and their seedlings are translocated to the truffle plantages.

It takes about 8-10 years for the mycorrhizal hyphae mats to develop and to bear truffles.

During that time the plantages have to be monitored, specifically, the soil has to be analyzed for potential competing fungi and bacteria.

As well as fenced and protected from wild boars, which dig up the soil and might damage the crop.

White truffle
(Tuber magnatum)

Fig. 27

Truffle cultivation dropped by 95-99% since the 19th century. The causes for it were the world wars and the industrialization, due to which many of the plots were repurposed and destroyed. It is important to note that France alone was responsible for 2000 tonnes of truffles per year during that period.

Planted truffle groves near Beaumont-du-Ventoux

Fig. 28

Truffles contain many volatile constituents (organic compounds, which have a low boiling point). Most of these constituents as well as the aromatic compounds are soluble in non-polar solutions (fats, oils, alcohols - yes, truffle vodka is a thing.)
Hence, most cooking with truffles is done via truffle oil or by addition to sauces (cream), for truffles by themselves have a very vague taste.

OTHER PEZIZALES SPECIES

Only to be found in specific locations in Japan and Texas.

Fig. 29

Devil's cigar
(Chorioactis geaster)

Hooded false morel
(Gyromitra infula)

Elfin saddle
(Helvella crispa)

Very rare, only found in Fennoskandia and 1 specimen in BC.

Witches cauldron
(Sarcosoma globosum)

(Caloscypha fulgens)

Described in 2002 by Finnish Mycologist Harri Harmaja.

Fig. 30   Fig. 31

LEOTIOMYCETA

Leotiomyceta is one of the biggest taxonomic groups in the Ascomycota division.

It is comprised of three important subdivisions:

Leotiomyceta
Dothideomyceta
Sordariomyceta

Phylum
ASCOMYCOTA

Subdivision
PEZIZOMYCOTINA
SACCHAROMYCOTINA
TAPHRINOMYCOTINA

PEZIZOMYCOTINA — **PEZIZOMYCETES**
LEOTIOMYCETA

LEOTIOMYCETA — **SORDARIOMYCETA**
DOTHIDEOMYCETA
LEOTIOMYCETES

DOTHIDEOMYCETA

Lichenized fungi, black yeasts, plant pathogens.

Fig.52

Fig.53

SORDARIOMYCETA

Insect pathogens.

Fig.54

LEOTIOMYCETES

Recently discovered, includes cyanolichens and elven cups.

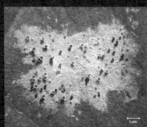
Fig.55

SORDARIOMYCETES

Sordariomycetes are a class in the subdivision Pezizomycotina. It is almost the largest class of Ascomycota, second to Pezizales.

in Latin 'sordes' stands for – filth, that's because some species grow in feces, however, most (not all) of the species in this class are pathogens and molds.
They can infect the stems, leaves, and roots of many different plants. However, insects can also become hosts for these creepy and fascinating fungi.

Subdivision
PEZIZOMYCOTINA ── **LEOTIOMYCETA**
└ **PEZIZOMYCETES**

LEOTIOMYCETA ── **SORDARIOMYCETA**
DOTHIDEOMYCETA
LEOTIOMYCETES

SORDARIOMYCOTA ── **SORDARIOMYCETES**

The categorization of Ascomycota is a bit awkward because many of them are microscopic, hard to distinguish, or live inside other organisms. This is the reason why identification is done mostly on a molecular level. Not that in Basidiomycota scientists wouldn't apply molecular methods (i.e. DNA analysis), but for some of them, identification based on morphological traits is reliable.

A lot of the phylogenetic relationships are still unresolved, hence many unranked subcategories appear and disappear while research is being conducted.

Another reason is their fast growth. In 2013, 600 genera and 3000 species were known. By 2015, it was 28 orders, 90 families, and 1344 genera. Now (2023) we are talking about 54 orders.

SORDARIOMYCETES ── **HYPOCREALES**
Class   Order

HYPOCREALES

Hypocreales species produce perithecial ascomata (ascocarp/ascoma is a fruiting body of an *Ascomycota* fungus, remember?). A perithecium is a flask-shaped fruiting body with a pore, also called an ostiole, for spore release.

Their ascomata are usually brightly colored – yellow, orange or red.

ASCOMYCOTA- CORDYCIPITACEAE

CORDYCIPITACEAE

The family of Cordycipitaceae is comprised of 21 genera, of which we will focus on 4 of them. They are insect pathogens with brightly colored and fleshy stromata. Fungal stromata, unlike in the botanical kingdom, are not any sort of openings, but rather a cushion of solid mycelium produced by many species - a hyphal modification.

Order **HYPOCREALES** —— Family **CORDYCIPITACEAE**

Stroma

Family **CORDYCIPITACEAE** —— Genus **CORDYCEPS**

CORDYCEPS

Up to 600 species that are distributed all over the world, of which many have a long history of use in Chinese medicine; some estimates date as far back as 1500 years.
Cordyceps species are endoparasitoids, living off of insects and arthropods (i.e. spiders)
The name stems from latin and ancient greek referring to its appearance -- clubheaded.

Most commonly cultivated on silk larva pupae, rice, and liquid nutrition.

Its active compound is cordycepin.

Cordyceps militaris

HEALTH BENEFITS

1. Male aphrodiziacum
2. Exercise performance
3. Anti-aging
4. Anti-tumor
5. Type II diabetes
6. Heart health
7. Anti-inflammatory

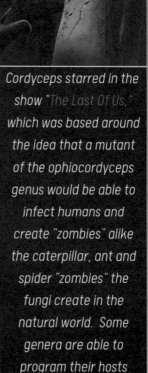

Cordyceps starred in the show "The Last Of Us," which was based around the idea that a mutant of the ophiocordyceps genus would be able to infect humans and create "zombies" alike the caterpillar, ant and spider "zombies" the fungi create in the natural world. Some genera are able to program their hosts behaviour, making them move to good spots for spore dispersal.

73

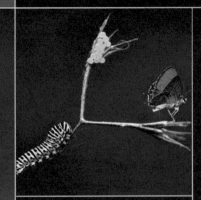

So, what most of you are asking yourself, I assume, is, how exactly do these fungi operate?

Beauveria has no fancy in-between mind-control games as ophiocordyceps (next page) has.

The conidia (sacky cells filled with spores) in most cases are airborne and thanks to the sheer number of them, they have a decent chance of landing on an insect somewhere along the way. Otherwise the insects might walk over them as well.

When they do, the spores germinate, grow hyphae and colonize the insects cuticle. When established, they sporulate again, repeating the cycle.

BEAUVERIA

Family
CORDYCIPITACEAE

Genus
CORDYCEPS
BEAUVERIA

This genus doesn't reproduce sexually, which when flipped to a human perspective, would be the same as if you split in two and created a clone of yourself, which if you ask me, is quite freaky.

Beauveria fungi are entomopathogenic, where 'ĕntomo' is Greek and stands for –insect, hence an insect pathogen. Fungi in this genus are white.

Now, per the idea of evolution, the clones do not remain the same for their entire lifespan. Their DNA morphs according to adaptations, which were necessary for their survival. By the time it splits again, and again, and again… it might be a different species from what it started as.

A cuticle is the outer layer, the shell of an insect. Fun fact: it is built with the same carbohydrate as fungi's outer layer is built with. Chitine (N-Acetylglucoseamine), which is undigestible for humans. (That's why we cook mushrooms!)

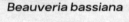

Beauveria bassiana

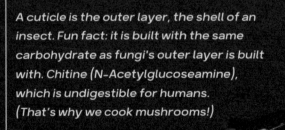

Fig. 36

ASCOMYCOTA- CORDYCIPITACEAE

GIBELLULA

The genus of Gibellula is specialized on arachnids, spiders.

Similar to Beauveria, Gibellula sends out spores, which then attach to an unlucky spider and germinate from inside.

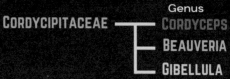

CORDYCIPITACEAE — Genus
CORDYCEPS
BEAUVERIA
GIBELLULA

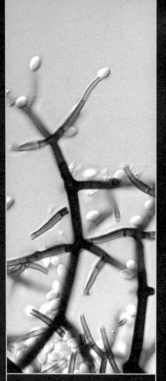

Gibellula pulchra

When a spider is infected, it will be slowly digested from inside out (by release of enzymes), which is sort of what spiders do to their prey so...jokes on you!

*This is called **external digestion**, since the digestive enzymes break down the organic material outside of the body of the consumer.*

The spiders are then engulfed in yellow mycelium, which after reaching maturity fades into a whitish grey and sporulates again.

not infected, just cute

Fungi imperfecti is a term which is used for fungi, which do not fit into the common definition of a species, similar to Beauveria, which reproduces asexually.

To be sexually compatible with another individual and produce fertile offspring is one of the key characteristics necessary to being identified as a species.

Fig. 37

75

OPHIOCORDYCIPITICEAE

Family of parasitic fungi with 12 genera and about 450 species.

Order	Family
HYPOCREALES	CORDYCIPITACEAE
	OPHIOCORDYCIPITICEAE

OPHIOCORDYCEPS

Often referred to as "zombie-ant fungi," have intruded into the imagination of many scientists and naturalists with their complex ecological interactions and potential applications in numerous fields.

They span from lush rainforests to arid grasslands across the globe.

Each of the species is parasitic and is hence specialized on a specific type of host organism and its environments. The mechanisms at play here are truly astonishing, and will make you reassess the intelligence of fungi.

Fig. 38

The fungus takes control over the ants brain and leads it to a tree nigh to the ants hill. The ant is forced to climb the tree, crawl on the underside of the leaf and bite down on one of its veins. Right there it is mummified, and when the fungus is mature, it releases its spores on the ant hill below.

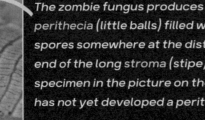

Fig. 38

The zombie fungus produces perithecia (little balls) filled with spores somewhere at the distal (far) end of the long stroma (stipe), the specimen in the picture on the right has not yet developed a perithecium.

Ophiocordyceps unilateralis

During the Himalayan gold rush, the _ophiocordyceps_ caterpillar fungus was collected en masse, driving the species to near extinction.

Considered as elusive and unique, for the fruiting body has yet to be sucessfully cultivated in laboratory conditions, hence, the only way to lay hands on this...

... jewel, is by embarking on expeditions into the mountains of Nepal, the Himalayas.

HEALTH BENEFITS

1. Male aphrodiziacum
2. Exercise performance
3. Anti-aging
4. Anti-tumor
5. Type II diabetes
6. Heart health
7. Anti-inflammatory

At the brisk of dawn, the mist still covering the leaf tips, local farmers will climb the hills to try their luck and look for this lucrative, sought-after, costly little caterpillar zombie.

For centuries it has been revered as a gift of healing by the population of the Tibetan plateaus.

The caterpillars, after infection, are forced to burry underground, where the fungus digests them and grows the stalk out of the dirt pile.

Its lucrativeness has brought the fungus almost to extinction, as it is considered endangered as of now.

Like the cordyceps militaris species, the active compound in this fungus is also cordycepin.

Ophiocordyceps sinensis

MOLDS & LICHENS

Although molds and lichens are not a separate phylogenetic group in the fungal kingdom, but rather structures that certain fungi implement, still I felt it would be of use to introduce them together, since the terms are such that are more broadly known and interacted with on a day-to-day basis.

Trichoderma longibrachiatum

Trichoderma longibrachiatum is a toxic mold fungus which causes strong allergic reactions in humans and animals alike. It can be found in blood samples of people with weak immune systems and causes nerve communication issues among other diseases.

The toxin trilongin is highly resistant to heat and detergents, hence the only way to deal with this fungus is prevention.

HYPOCREACEAE

The family consists of about 17 genera and 658 species, of which many have complex sexual reproductive cycles and produce medicinal but also toxic metabolites.

Order
HYPOCREALES

Family
CORDYCIPITACEAE
OPHIOCORDYCIPITICEAE
HYPOCREACEAE

TRICHODERMA

Trichoderma is a genus whose species are present in all soils around the world. Besides prevailing in the soil, some of them are identified as opportunistic avirulent (non-pathogenic) plant symbionts.

The fungi contain enzymes that break down cellulose and chitin. Cellulose is present in plant matter, hence they can thrive on wood and bark, however, their chitin enzymes imply, that indeed, Trichoderma sp. can decompose the cell walls of other fungi.

Trichoderma viride

T. viride is a biofungicide, which is used for protection of soils from pathogens caused by other fungi, such as Fusarium and Armillaria.

Molds are most of the time portrayed on petri dishes, which are small plastic bowls filled with yummy sugar-potato substrate.

Trichoderma alutaceum

ASCOMYCOTA - HYPOCREACEAE

HYPOMYCES

"Why is there a mushroom in the mold section?" you might ask yourself. Well, that's because it is a mold that grows on fungi!

The genus of *Hypomyces* is comprised of a handful of species, of which all are parasites that decompose and digest fungal biomass.

And to your surprise, yes, the lobster mushroom is edible and is considered a delicacy in some countries. Especially, if the mold grows over milk-caps, it counteracts the spicy flavour of the milk-cap, making it more enjoyable.

Order
HYPOCREALES

Family
CORDYCIPITACEAE
OPHIOCORDYCIPITICEAE
HYPOCREACEAE

So what you see here is a russulales species covered in an orange mold fungus, the lobster mushroom.

Hypomyces cervinigenus

Fig. 39

The two other hypomyces species are parasites on the Helvella (Elf saddle, upper picture) and Boletus (porcino, lower picture) species.

Lobster mushroom
(*Hypomyces lactifluorum*)

The lobster mushroom can be found on brittlegills and milk-caps in North America and has been spotted on a market in Oregon.

Bolete eater
(*Hypomyces chrysospermus*)

Fig. 40

81

ASCOMYCOTA - NECTRIACEAE

Nectriopsis violaceae

Fig. 41

NECTRIACEAE

A family of about 70 genera and 1336 species with a more prominent presence in tropical and warm regions, however, don't be fooled, genera such as *Fusarium* are prevalent also in temperate regions, causing mischief.

Order	Family
HYPOCREALES	CORDYCIPITACEAE
	OPHIOCORDYCIPITICEAE
	HYPOCREACEAE
	NECTRIACEAE

Family	Genus
NECTRIACEAE	FUSARIUM

FUSARIUM

Fusarium is a plant pathogen. The infection with *Fusarium* is termed FHB, fusarium head blight (seen on the picture on the next page, the purple discoloration).

The FHB devastates crops such as wheat, barley, maize and rice, causing economic damage up to billions.

Consumption of the mycotoxins released during infection can cause vomiting, liver damage and fertility defects.

Slime mold (Fuligo septica)

Bionectriaceae is a family in the order Hypocreales. Nectriopsis violaceae can be seen on the picture above growing on Fuligo septica - a slime mold. Slime molds are not fungi, they are a clump of individual cells working in unison.

Nectria cinnabarina, the coral spot, is a plant pathogen which causes blisters as seen below. It will predate parasitically on stressed trees or decompose dead ones.

Fusarium solani

Fusarium graminearum

Coral spot (Nectria cinnabarina)

DOTHIDEOMYCETA

Is a rankless taxon, which is currently unaccepted, but has been used as an umbrella taxon for *Dothideomycetes, Eurotiomycetes* and *Lecanoromycetes* in several studies.

LEOTIOMYCETA
- SORDARIOMYCETA
- **DOTHIDEOMYCETA**
- LEOTIOMYCETES

DOTHIDEOMYCETA
- DOTHIDEOMYCETES
- EUROTIOMYCETES
- LECANOROMYCETES

LECANOROMYCETES

I present to you, the largest class of lichenized fungi.

"What was lichen again?"

A symbiotic relationship between fungi and algae.

"Algae?"

Yup.

This class is filled with lots of uncategorized genera, the precise relationships are yet to be determined.

You see... it is always the small stuff that is difficult to identify. (gotcha!)

It is hypothesized that this symbiosis is the product of fungi aiding plants to climb out of the ocean onto solid ground.

LECANOROMYCETES —— RHIZOCARPALES

RHIZOCARPALES

An order comprised, by the most part, of crustose lichens (lichens, which form a very rigid outer crust, which can only be separated from its substrate by scraping it off, hence destroying the lichen).

The maximum surface area of the lichens growing on the rock is averaged, and with a given growth size, the date of colonization can be determined.

This fungus is applied in determining the relative age of debri and minerals, helping understand glacial advances.

This application is called lichenometry, and is based on the assumption that the lichen growing on the rock is the oldest organism.

The map lichen
(*Rhizocarpon geographicum*)

ASCOMYCOTA - DOTHIDEOMYCETA

DOTHIDEOMYCETES

Dothideomycetes are the largest class of Ascomycota with a wide variety of fungi. It includes 11 orders, 90 families, 1300 genera, and 19000 species.

The best known species of this class are infamous plant pathogens.

Stagnospora nodorum is reponsible for the Septoria nodorum blotch.

The long needle like hairs are hyphae growing out of the plant, they dig into the cells or enter through the pores (stomata, little openings in leaves, through which gases are exchanged with the environment).

Serves as a model organism for fungicide research.

DOTHIDEOMYCETA ── DOTHIDEOMYCETES
EUROTIOMYCETES
LECANOROMYCETES

DOTHIDEOMYCETES ── PLEOSPOLARES
PLEOSPORALES ── PHAEOSPHAERIACEAE

PLEOSPORALES

The biggest order of the Dothideomycetes (a real mouthful, huh?)

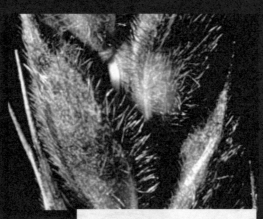

Stagnospora nodorum

Alternaria sp. conidia

It harbors, by old estimates, 23 families, 332 genera and about 4700 species. Their habitats range from fresh water to marine as well as terrestrial.

Although mostly saprobic, some species live as parasites, epiphytes, and endophytes.

hosts: bunts, smuts

Although some pathogens won't kill their hosts, Alternaria doesn't provide such favors. Such pathogens are known as "necrotrophic".

Causes the black spot disease.

hosts: cabbages, oil plants, broccoli and more.

And although these specimens are plant pathogens, when breathed in by humans, they can contribute to the development of respiratory sicknesses.

Alternaria brassicicola

85

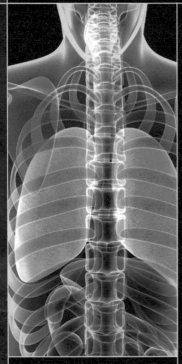

DIDYMELLACEAE

PLEOSPORALES — PHAEOSPHAERIACEAE
DIDYMELLACEAE

Rather little known is about this family. It can be found across the globe and has recently been reorganized. It harbors many odd-named, to the general public unknown, genera. However, one of them I felt was necessary to introduce.

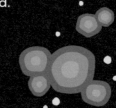

EPICOCCUM   DIDYMELLACEAE —— EPICOCCUM

Epicoccum is a mold fungus which grows on... other fungi!

It has a dark brown-green colour and its colonies grow quickly.

It grows also in soil, peat, leaf litter, humus, sewages etc.

Since it grows on other fungi it has evolved many molecules which are of significant use in medicine and biotechnology.

Epicoccum nigrum

The antimicrobial chemicals produced by Epicoccum are used in the fight against other harmful fungi and bacteria present in soil, so in example Flavipin and Epicocconone.

Attempted to be used in production of antibiotics.

Its pigments are used to color food!

Used against brown rot in stone fruits.

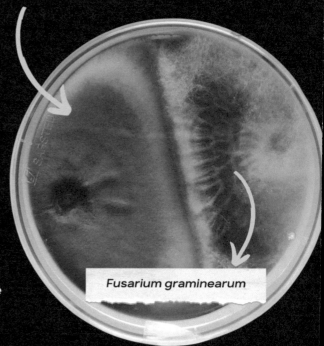

Fusarium graminearum

When living in with Epicoccum infested rooms, one is exposed to the danger of respiratory fungal allergies such as asthma, pneumonitis, fungal sinusitis and hypersensitivity pneumonitis. It cross reacts with other fungal allergens, meaning, if in presence of other specific species it can cause other unexpected health issues such as compromising ones immune system.

EUROTIOMYCETES

The third class of the *Dothideomyceta*, the *Eurotiomycetes*.

The third largest lichenized class.

From estimated 3810 species, about 1200 are lichens.

DOTHIDEOMYCETA ——
- DOTHIDEOMYCETES
- LECANOROMYCETES
- EUROTIOMYCETES

EUROTIOMYCETES —— **EUROTIALES**

The fruiting bodies, ascocarps, of *Eurotiomycetes* are, for the most part, cleisthothecia.

EUROTIALES

An order comprised of blue and green mold fungi.

EUROTIALES —— **TRICHOCOMACEAE**

TRICHOCOMACEAE

39 known genera of saprobic fungi, living off of dead matter, which are able to adapt to the harshest of conditions.

Aspergillus sp. grows, like Epicoccum, in a broad range of habitats: soil, leaf litter, water, vegetation etc.

The fact that Aspergillus is a rapid growth fungus puts it in the category of species suited for biological research.

Besides the fact it grows fast, it is able to produce (synthesise) large quantities of secondary metabolites

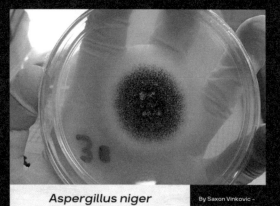

Aspergillus niger

Fig. 42

By Saxon Vinkovic – Own work, CC BY-SA 4.0, https://commons.wiki media.org/w/index.ph p?curid:73626248

Secondary metabolites are compounds used for, i.e. interactions with an organism's environment, not essential for survival).

Some of those metabolites are citric acid (the sour taste in lemons is due to citric acid), and gluconic acid, which is used for cleaning, laying cement or as an additive in medication.

Some of you might have guessed already... secondary metabolites, interacting with the environment... toxic compounds?

Aspergillus niger produces mycotoxins, called ochratoxins and can grow both, as a plant pathogen (see picture of Aspergillus growing on an onion) and as a human pathogen.

When consumed from food it can cause kidney failure and cancer.

When it grows in humans it can cause aspergillosis on the skin and in the lungs. Can be fatal.

Drosophila melanogaster

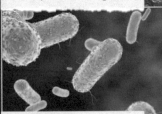
Escherichia coli

Arabidopsis thaliana

Model species are species which are used in genetics to conduct in-depth genetic research to learn more about other species. Model species are chosen on a basis of multiple factors, of which one are short life cycles, because, to wait 50 years for an organism to reach maturity and see the impact of a modification is not... smart, especially when at optimum conditions a fruit fly needs 19 days to reach full maturity.

SORDARIALES

One of the most diverse orders in the *Sordariomycetes* class. Their ascomata (spore sacks) are motly perithecial (cup-shaped) and most of them are saprobic (growing on decomposing matter in absence of oxygen).

NEUROSPORA

Neurospora is a red bread mold, its name stems from stripes on its hyphaes which makes them resemble nerve cells (Neuro - nerve, Spora - spore).
Neurospora is a fungal model organism, found in tropical and subtropical regions (especialy after forest fires).
It has 7 chromosomes (10 000 genes) of which all have been sequenced.

Subdivision
PEZIZOMYCOTINA — PEZIZALES
SORDARIOMYCETES

Class
SORDARIOMYCETES — HYPOCREALES
SORDARIALES

Order
SORDARIALES — **Family**
SORDARIACEAE

SORDARIACEAE

A family which harbors some very common molds, which you can find at home, but also important model species used for genetic research.

Fig. 43

Neurospora crassa

A Nobel prize was won in a study with Neurospora. In the study, it was x-rayed, which caused mutations, which caused failure in metabolic pathways because of errors in enzyme functions.

This gave birth to the 1 enzyme 1 gene hypothesis, which says that specific genes code for specific enzymes.

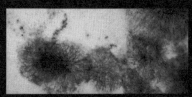

ASCOMYCOTA - SORDARIACEAE

SORDARIA

Although commonly found in herbivore feces, the genus *Sordaria* can also grow in soil, decaying plant matter and symbiotically with some plants.

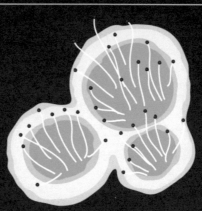

The species *Sordaria fimicola* can be found across the globe.

It grows black perithecia on white mycelial 'stems', giving the usually gray or green fluffy mold a dotted pattern.

The species Sordaria fimicola can be found across the globe.

In the picture of *Sordaria fimicola* a peculiar situation is taking place. In introduction to laboratory mycology work students are often asked to grow cultures of *Sordaria fimicola*, however, one of them is wild and the other a mutant. The wild types are mostly dark brown, as where the mutants are grey. If the mycelia are compatible they will produce offspring, which is then observed for the preservation of color, which gives us hints at the events taken place during the crossing over phase of meiosis, where ends of a chromosome of each partner are switched.

Fig. 44

Sordaria fimicola

Certain yeasts are the cause of some of the most common human infections. Yeats are present on the human skin and in our gut as part of a healthy and normal microbiome, however if the balance is disturbed the yeast can overgrow and cause an infection.

Most common human yeast infections are caused by a genus candida. The infections can occur inside the body or outside for example on the finger nails.

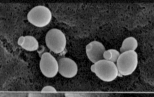

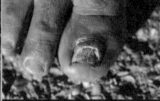

Candida albicans

SACCHAROMYCOTINA "TRUE YEASTS"

Did you know that yeast is a fungus?
Saccharomycotina is a subdivision of *Ascomycota* that encases most of the yeasts. Yeasts don't form a single taxonomic unit. Instead, some yeasts belong to *Basidiomycota*, and the rest, called "true yeasts," belong to Ascomycota.

Yeasts use organic compounds such as sugars as energy to grow. Therefore naturally, yeasts occur on sugar-rich surfaces such as fruit skins. Yeasts are unicellular organisms that have 3-5 microns in diameter and a lifespan of a few days.

Yeasts usually reproduce by budding. In budding the mother cells form knobs that separate from the mother cell forming new cells. This is very different from molds which grow hyphae . Some fungi do both of these and are called dimorphic fungi

ASCOMYCOTA
- PEZIZOMYCOTINA
- **SACCHAROMYCOTINA**
- TAPHRINOMYCOTINA

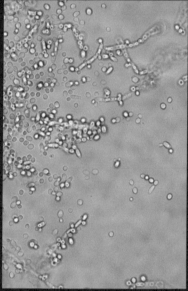

Yeasts can grow in the absence of oxygen, anaerobically, but also in presence of oxygen. They are obligate anaerobes.

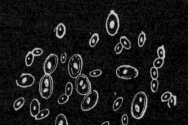

ASCOMYCOTA - SACCHAROMYCOTA

Yeast is a great example of fungi's potential in biotechnology.
Humankind has been able to utilize its fermentation properties around the same time as the beginning of agriculture.
New uses of yeasts have been discovered in recent years.

Yeast Candida tropicalis is used to produce xylitol in a chemical reaction.

Xylitol can be found in chewing gum and it may help prevent caries – dental cavities.

Yeast converts sugar from the mixture to alcohol and carbon dioxide. The name "Yeast" originates from Old English where 'gist' means 'foam' or 'bubble'. It has been used in alcohol making long before we knew what it actually was.

There is more to yeasts than just its use in the kitchen. New research has shown promising results in the microbial biofuel industry.
In the same way as yeasts produce alcohol during fermentation of beer and wine, the ethanol could be harnessed to generate electricity in the form of a biofuel.

Saccharomycotina yeasts are probably one of the first domesticated organisms. They have been utilized in baking and alcohol-brewing very early in human history (even 10 000 years ago).
The most common commercial yeast, the Bakers yeast has been sold since 1780.

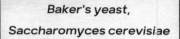
Baker's yeast, Saccharomyces cerevisiae

Taphrinomycotina includes also some yeasts in the class *Schizosaccharomyces*. These are fission yeasts which means that instead of budding they reproduce by fission (splitting in the middle).

Fission is when the rod-shaped cells separate to two equal sized daughter cells by splitting in the middle.

Fission yeast is an important model organism in studying genetics and cellular procesess since the end of 18th century.

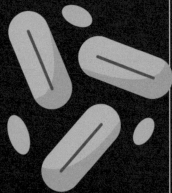

TAPHRINOMYCOTINA

ASCOMYCOTA
- PEZIZOMYCOTINA
- SACCHAROMYCOTINA
- TAPHRINOMYCOTINA

Taphrinomycotina is the last of the three subdivisions of *Ascomycota*. Including the classes *Archaeorhizomycetes*, *Neolectomycetes*, *Pneumocystidomycetes*, *Schizosaccharomycetes* and *Taphrinomycetes*

Fig. 45

Taphrinomycetes are plant parasites which infect mostly plant leaves, catkins and branches.
They have two separate developmental stages: a yeast stage and a filamentous hyphal stage. Organisms with two different states are called dimorphic.

Archaeorhizomycetes are plant symbionts in the *Taphrinomycotina* subdivision. These fungi prefer coniferous trees, and their main hosts are hemlocks, spruces, pines, and heathers. The relationship between the symbiont (the fungi) and host (the tree) is so far classified as neither parasitic nor mycorrhizal. However, the *Archaeorhizomycetes* are a relatively new discovery (20 years) and there are many more species to be found in the future. They don't have fruiting bodies or spores.

Pneumocystidomycetes

Pneumocystidomycetes include only a few species in the family of *Pneumocystis*. They are yeast-like fungi that live as parasites in animals. Each species has its own specific host : *P. carinii* and *P. wakefieldidae* infect rats, *P. murina* infects mice and *P. oryctolagi* infects rabbits. These different fungi species cannot infect other animals than their specific host that they have co-evolved with.

The most known species is the *Pneumocystis jirovecii* which is a parasite of humans.

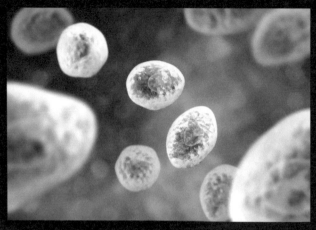

The host cells of Pneumocystis turns into cysts that holds the new spores inside.

It infects the lungs of significantly immunocompromised people, causing so-called Pneumocystis pneumonia. In people with a normally functioning immune system, *P. jirovecii* is quite a common and silent infection.

Neolectomycetes - Neolectaceae

The *Neolectaceae* fungi are the only *Ascomycota* fungi outside the *Pezizomycotina* subdivision that form visible fruiting bodies. The yellow club-shaped and smooth fruiting bodies share the name Earth tongues with a few other *Ascomycetes* e.g. *Geoglossum* and *Microglossum*

The velvety earthtongue
(*Trichoglossum hirsutum*)

Neolecta irregularis

BONUS: A BACHELOR THESIS IN MYCOLOGY

During my studies at a University in Germany, I worked on leaf litter fungi from the local woods, some of which you heard about in the previous pages. The goal was to study fungal interactions, hoping to find a way to suppress crop blights such as *Fusarium*.

They were grown on different media and in different temperatures, however, in pairs. The fungal version of the roman gladiator arena, if you will... battle to the death.

Some species could thwart the growth of their opponents, even without physical contact, meaning the fungus had to recognize that the competing fungus was close and acted accordingly by releasing inhibiting molecules through gas or agar (discoloration visible).

Of all of the fungi, Fusarium proved to be the most vicious and adaptable. It grew fast in warm and colder conditions. In terms of colonized area, it often outgrew its competitor.

However, Epicoccum nigrum, seemed to implement a different strategy, as it did not grow as explosively, rather, once it reached maturity, it released its spores which germinated on the competing fungus, ultimately winning.

Brown discoloration – release of volatile compounds.

Epicoccum overgrowing Penicillium

Epicoccum overgrowing Fusarium

Epicoccum overgrowing Sordaria

THANK YOU.

Thank you for not only supporting our work but also making it through. We encourage you to join us on our Facebook page and share your thoughts and opinions about the book.

Criticism, suggestions, and ideas are all welcome.

We would also like to encourage you to send us a picture of you and your favorite mushroom, which we would like to include either in the second edition of this book or in Book 2: Fungal Ecology & Cell Biology (if there is a desire for such a book).

The best way to support our work and show us you'd like to see book 2 is to leave us a review on Amazon, as those are hard to come by.

We want to give away a mushroom coloring book and a little mushroom surprise box to the first five of you.

(Simply send us a message.) We would love to hear from you!!

MUSHROOM TROPHIES

FB PAGE

Scan or type in:
bit.ly/AuthorHJK

AMAZON

Scan or type in:
bit.ly/AmazonHJK

UPCOMING PROJECTS

A fantasy and sci-fi novel about a young mycologist who will have to navigate his way through the Amazon jungle and his own pensive mind, while fighting a new age war no one expected.

I am writing this live on wildw.substack.com

where you can read it for free. (A lot of editing and rebuilding will be done before the book is finished.)

Our biology/comic book series will be continued eventually. We are planning to hire professionals to do the illustrations.

MUSHROOM
ADULT COLORING BOOK

Soon available on amazon.

SUPER SMART FUNGUS VOL.2

ATTRIBUTIONS - PHOTOS & ILLUSTRATIONS

FIG.1 BIOLOGY 2E. PROVIDED BY: OPENSTAX. LOCATED AT: HTTPS://OPENSTAX.ORG/DETAILS/BOOKS/BIOLOGY-2E. LICENSE: CC BY: ATTRIBUTION. LICENSE TERMS: DOWNLOAD FOR FREE AT HTTP://CNX.ORG/CONTENTS/8D50A0AF-948B-4204-A71D-4826CBA765B8@8.19

FIG.2 BY JEAN PAUL <BILLYJOLLY@WANADOO.FR> - HTTP://PECHE-MOUCHE-SECHE.COM/SECHEGRAISSE_FICHIERS/IMAGE006.JPG, CC BY-SA 4.0, HTTPS://COMMONS.WIKIMEDIA.ORG/W/INDEX.PHP?CURID=35188169

FIG.3 BY ALEX EX, CC BY-SA 4.0 <HTTPS://CREATIVECOMMONS.ORG/LICENSES/BY-SA/4.0>, VIA WIKIMEDIA COMMONS

FIG.4 BY STEPH JARVIS - THIS IMAGE IS IMAGE NUMBER 483579 AT MUSHROOM OBSERVER, A SOURCE FOR MYCOLOGICAL IMAGES., CC BY-SA 3.0, HTTPS://COMMONS.WIKIMEDIA.ORG/W/INDEX.PHP?CURID=36869926

FIG.5 BY THIS IMAGE WAS CREATED BY USER (HRÍB) AT MUSHROOM OBSERVER, A SOURCE FOR MYCOLOGICAL IMAGES.YOU CAN CONTACT THIS USER HERE. - THIS IMAGE IS IMAGE NUMBER 49357 AT MUSHROOM OBSERVER, A SOURCE FOR MYCOLOGICAL IMAGES., CC BY-SA 3.0, HTTPS://COMMONS.WIKIMEDIA.ORG/W/INDEX.PHP?CURID=7978137

FIG.6 BY JASON HOLLINGER - ROSY POLYPOREUPLOADED BY AMADA44, CC BY 2.0, HTTPS://COMMONS.WIKIMEDIA.ORG/W/INDEX.PHP?CURID=24213704

FIG.7 BY AGNES MONKELBAAN - OWN WORK, CC BY-SA 4.0, HTTPS://COMMONS.WIKIMEDIA.ORG/W/INDEX.PHP?CURID=79721717

FIG.8 HTTPS://WWW.FORESTFLOORNARRATIVE.COM/BLOG/2018/1/12/FUNGI-FRIDAY-A-GILLED-TROPICAL-POLYPORE-LENTINUS-BERTEROI

FIG.9 BY EICHHASE.JPG: LEBRACDERIVATIVE WORK: AK CCM - THIS FILE WAS DERIVED FROM: EICHHASE.JPG:, CC BY-SA 3.0, HTTPS://COMMONS.WIKIMEDIA.ORG/W/INDEX.PHP?CURID=20591468

FIG.10 BY STEPHEN RUSSELL (MYCOTA) - THIS IMAGE IS IMAGE NUMBER 119220 AT MUSHROOM OBSERVER, A SOURCE FOR MYCOLOGICAL IMAGES., CC BY-SA 3.0, HTTPS://COMMONS.WIKIMEDIA.ORG/W/INDEX.PHP?CURID=18554513

FIG.11 BY Σ64 - OWN WORK, CC BY 3.0, HTTPS://COMMONS.WIKIMEDIA.ORG/W/INDEX.PHP?CURID=36080658

FIG.12 BY THIS IMAGE WAS CREATED BY USER NATHAN WILSON (NATHAN) AT MUSHROOM OBSERVER, A SOURCE FOR MYCOLOGICAL IMAGES.YOU CAN CONTACT THIS USER HERE. - THIS IMAGE IS IMAGE NUMBER 153 AT MUSHROOM OBSERVER, A SOURCE FOR MYCOLOGICAL IMAGES., CC BY-SA 3.0, HTTPS://COMMONS.WIKIMEDIA.ORG/W/INDEX.PHP?CURID=20257728

FIG.13 BY JASON HOLLINGER - WHITE CHEESE POLYPOREUPLOADED BY AMADA44, CC BY 2.0, HTTPS://COMMONS.WIKIMEDIA.ORG/W/INDEX.PHP?CURID=24216572

FIG.14 BY DAN MOLTER, CC BY-SA 3.0, HTTPS://COMMONS.WIKIMEDIA.ORG/W/INDEX.PHP?CURID=6582603

FIG.15 BY DICK CULBERT FROM GIBSONS, B.C., CANADA - FAVOLUS TENUICULUS, CC BY 2.0, HTTPS://COMMONS.WIKIMEDIA.ORG/W/INDEX.PHP?CURID=50660885

FIG.16 BY PETAR MILOŠEVIĆ - OWN WORK, CC BY-SA 4.0, HTTPS://COMMONS.WIKIMEDIA.ORG/W/INDEX.PHP?CURID=62909769

FIG.17 BY © HANS HILLEWAERT, CC BY-SA 4.0, HTTPS://COMMONS.WIKIMEDIA.ORG/W/INDEX.PHP?CURID=15504239

FIG.18 BY ALAN ROCKEFELLER - THIS IMAGE IS IMAGE NUMBER 283494 AT MUSHROOM OBSERVER, A SOURCE FOR MYCOLOGICAL IMAGES., CC BY-SA 3.0, HTTPS://COMMONS.WIKIMEDIA.ORG/W/INDEX.PHP?CURID=22759856

FIG.19 BY THIS IMAGE WAS CREATED BY USER CHRISTINE BRAATEN (WINTERSBEFORE) AT MUSHROOM OBSERVER, A SOURCE FOR MYCOLOGICAL IMAGES.YOU CAN CONTACT THIS USER HERE. - THIS IMAGE IS IMAGE NUMBER 345428 AT MUSHROOM OBSERVER, A SOURCE FOR MYCOLOGICAL IMAGES., CC BY-SA 3.0, HTTPS://COMMONS.WIKIMEDIA.ORG/W/INDEX.PHP?CURID=36766876

FIG.20 BY JENS HENRIK PETERSEN - BY EMAIL. IMAGE ALSO AVAILABLE AT HTTP://WWW.MYCOKEY.ORG/RESULTFIND.SHTML?GENSPEC=SPECIES&ID=911&14872, CC BY-SA 3.0, HTTPS://COMMONS.WIKIMEDIA.ORG/W/INDEX.PHP?CURID=40317371

FIG.21 BY HTTPS://WWW.INATURALIST.ORG/PEOPLE/TARASEVERNS - HTTPS://WWW.INATURALIST.ORG/PHOTOS/248173609, CC BY 4.0, HTTPS://COMMONS.WIKIMEDIA.ORG/W/INDEX.PHP?CURID=126956330

FIG.22 BY USER TIM SAGE (T. SAGE) AT MUSHROOM OBSERVER, A SOURCE FOR MYCOLOGICAL IMAGES. YOU CAN CONTACT THIS USER HERE. - THIS IMAGE IS IMAGE NUMBER 681401 AT MUSHROOM OBSERVER, A SOURCE FOR MYCOLOGICAL IMAGES., CC BY-SA 3.0, HTTPS://COMMONS.WIKIMEDIA.ORG/W/INDEX.PHP?CURID=54323222

FIG.23 BY I. G. SAFONOV (IGSAFONOV) - THIS IMAGE IS IMAGE NUMBER 56647 AT MUSHROOM OBSERVER, A SOURCE FOR MYCOLOGICAL IMAGES., CC BY-SA 3.0

FIG.24 BY DEBIVORT, CC BY-SA 3.0, HTTPS://COMMONS.WIKIMEDIA.ORG/W/INDEX.PHP?CURID=865503

FIG.25 BY ILMARI KARONEN - OWN WORK, CC BY 3.0

FIG.26 BY VAYSSIE ROBERT ROBERT VAYSSIé - OWN WORKGIGNAC LOT FRANCE, CC BY-SA 3.0

FIG.27 BY MATTHIAS KABEL - OWN WORK, CC BY-SA 3.0

FIG.28 BY MARIANNE CASAMANCE - OWN WORK, CC BY-SA 3.0

FIG.29 BY TIM JONES - HTTP://WWW.GROUNDTRUTHINVESTIGATIONS.ORG/PHOTOGRAPHY/FLORA/FUNGI/DEV_CIGAR.HTML, CC BY 3.0

FIG.30 BY TIM JONES - HTTP://WWW.GROUNDTRUTHINVESTIGATIONS.ORG, CC BY 3.0

FIG.31 BY STAFFAN KYRK - OWN WORK, CC BY 3.0

FIG.32 BY THIS IMAGE WAS CREATED BY USER JASON KARAKEHIAN (JASON KARAKEHIAN) AT MUSHROOM OBSERVER, A SOURCE FOR MYCOLOGICAL IMAGES.YOU CAN CONTACT THIS USER HERE. - THIS IMAGE IS IMAGE NUMBER 159063 AT MUSHROOM OBSERVER, A SOURCE FOR MYCOLOGICAL IMAGES., CC BY-SA 3.0,

FIG.33 BY RASBAK - OWN WORK, CC BY-SA 3.0

FIG.34 BY SUHAIB FIRDOUS YATOO - MYCOPORTAL, CC BY-SA 3.0

FIG.35   BY HEIZER - OWN WORK, CC BY-SA 3.0

FIG.36   BY THIS IMAGE WAS CREATED BY USER DANNY NEWMAN (NEWMY51) AT MUSHROOM OBSERVER, A SOURCE FOR MYCOLOGICAL IMAGES.YOU CAN CONTACT THIS USER HERE. - THIS IMAGE IS IMAGE NUMBER 16552 AT MUSHROOM OBSERVER, A SOURCE FOR MYCOLOGICAL IMAGES., CC BY-SA 3.0, HTTPS://COMMONS.WIKIMEDIA.ORG/W/INDEX.PHP?CURID=8355082

FIG.37   BY SUHAIB FIRDOUS YATOO - MYCOPORTAL, CC BY-SA 3.0, HTTPS://COMMONS.WIKIMEDIA.ORG/W/INDEX.PHP?CURID=105543591

FIG.38   BY DAVID P. HUGHES, MAJ-BRITT PONTOPPIDAN - HTTPS://JOURNALS.PLOS.ORG/PLOSONE/ARTICLE?ID=10.1371/JOURNAL.PONE.0004835, CC BY 2.5, HTTPS://COMMONS.WIKIMEDIA.ORG/W/INDEX.PHP?CURID=17917778

FIG.39   BY SAVA KRSTIC (SAVA) - THIS IMAGE IS IMAGE NUMBER 487195 AT MUSHROOM OBSERVER, A SOURCE FOR MYCOLOGICAL IMAGES., CC BY-SA 3.0, HTTPS://COMMONS.WIKIMEDIA.ORG/W/INDEX.PHP?CURID=37077054

FIG.40   BY SASATA - OWN WORK, CC BY-SA 3.0, HTTPS://COMMONS.WIKIMEDIA.ORG/W/INDEX.PHP?CURID=8386339

FIG.41   BY DICK CULBERT FROM GIBSONS, B.C., CANADA - NECTRIOPSIS VIOLACEA, CC BY 2.0, HTTPS://COMMONS.WIKIMEDIA.ORG/W/INDEX.PHP?CURID=50655984

FIG.42   BY SAXON VINKOVIC - OWN WORK, CC BY-SA 4.0, HTTPS://COMMONS.WIKIMEDIA.ORG/W/INDEX.PHP?CURID=73626248

FIG.43   BY ROLAND GROMES - OWN WORK, CC BY-SA 3.0, HTTPS://COMMONS.WIKIMEDIA.ORG/W/INDEX.PHP?CURID=25292689

FIG.44   BY NINJATACOSHELL - OWN WORK, CC BY-SA 3.0, HTTPS://COMMONS.WIKIMEDIA.ORG/W/INDEX.PHP?CURID=6778290

FIG.45   BY GIANCARLO DESSÌ - OWN WORK, CC BY-SA 3.0, HTTPS://COMMONS.WIKIMEDIA.ORG/W/INDEX.PHP?CURID=4072350

FIG.46   BY USER WALT STURGEON (MYCOWALT) AT MUSHROOM OBSERVER, A SOURCE FOR MYCOLOGICAL IMAGES.YOU CAN CONTACT THIS USER HERE. - THIS IMAGE IS IMAGE NUMBER 76559 AT MUSHROOM OBSERVER, A SOURCE FOR MYCOLOGICAL IMAGES., CC BY-SA 3.0, HTTPS://COMMONS.WIKIMEDIA.ORG/W/INDEX.PHP?CURID=11693689

MANY THANKS TO EVERYONE WHO POSTED THEIR PICTURES FOR FREE USE ON THE INTERNET, IF YOU'RE ONE OF THE CONTRIBUTORS, PLEASE SEND US A MESSAGE.

COVER ART DONE BY SABRINA CARBALLO AND HER TEAM ESABFC.

Made in United States
Troutdale, OR
09/28/2024

23219860R00062